SOME DISSENTING VOICES

SOME DISSENTING VOICES

The Story of Six American Dissenters

Arthur and Lila Weinberg

The World Publishing Company
New York and Cleveland

Published by The World Publishing Company
110 East 59th Street, New York, New York 10022

Published simultaneously in Canada by
Nelson, Foster & Scott Ltd.

Library of Congress catalog card number: 78–128525

Printed in the United States of America.

For

Hedy, Anita, and Wendy
and their contemporaries
Dissenters with a Cause

CONTENTS

Always the Challenge 11

Lincoln Steffens
Muckraker and Journalist 17

Eugene Victor Debs
Labor Organizer and Socialist 53

Clarence Seward Darrow
Lawyer and Humanist 85

John Peter Altgeld
Statesman and Democrat 119

Jane Addams
Social Worker and World Citizen 147

Robert Green Ingersoll
Agnostic and Republican 175

The Challenge Continues 207

Acknowledgments and Suggested Readings 209

Index 218

SOME DISSENTING VOICES

ALWAYS THE CHALLENGE

THE DISSENTERS in this book spoke with presidents and dictators, farmers and workers, senators and political activists. They were movers and shakers in an age in which men challenged tradition but never really dislodged it. They were protesters who gave others courage to question, to believe, to hope, to act. They were the conscience of their times.

Their lifetimes spanned more than a century of war and peace, revolution and counterrevolution, depression and prosperity. During this period the agrarian-commercial society of the United States gave way to the rise of industrialization as the nation grew from twenty-four states to forty-eight, passed through twenty-six presidential elections from Andrew Jackson to Franklin Delano Roosevelt, engaged in the Civil War, the Spanish-American War, World War I, saw the beginning of World War II, and changed from a policy of isolationism to the acceptance of its role as a world power.

From 1833 to 1938, during the lives of these six dissenters, the workday was shortened from fourteen hours to eight, child labor was outlawed, and legislation was passed to protect women working in factories and shops. Labor organization became a force in the life of the nation as big business met with trade unions in collective bargaining negotiations. Slavery was abolished, but dignity and equality were still denied to the black man.

These years covered the period of laissez faire capitalism in which big business ruthlessly dominated the political and economic scene, and continued through the era of the muckrakers who exposed the corruption of society and acted as publicity men for reform.

This was the age of reform: Populism with its demand for equal rights, with its hostility to concentrated economic power and its setting of human rights against property rights; Progressivism with its anti-monopoly and social reforms; all culminating in the election of Franklin Delano Roosevelt, who as President encouraged a depressed nation that it had nothing to fear but fear itself and then proposed social and economic legislation which had been urged earlier by most of the dissenting voices in this volume.

In the 105 years which make up the lifetimes of the six rebels in this book, women's suffrage was enacted, prohibition was passed and repealed, and the clergy reexamined the teachings of their churches as these related to social and economic questions. The clash between Darwinism and Fundamentalism reached popular recognition with the Scopes trial in Dayton, Tennessee, when John T. Scopes, a high school teacher, discussed Charles Darwin's theory of evolution in his classroom. During this period, there also emerged on

American soil the struggle between the ideologies of the Russian anarchist Michael Bakunin and the German Socialist Karl Marx.

Anarchism as a criticism of the political state is as old as recorded history. America has always had antistatist philosophers. Philosophical anarchism is found in the political thinking of Thomas Jefferson, Henry David Thoreau, Ralph Waldo Emerson, and Josiah Warren.

The social doctrine of anarchism as a political movement, however, preaching direct action, strikes, protest, even violence, reached the United States in the late 1870's during a period of intense labor unrest. Though socialism had already appeared on the American scene, it never aroused the fear of the Establishment as did anarchism. Many of the anarchists were dissidents from the Socialist movement; they questioned the importance of the State, challenged authority, and turned away from political action as a way to solve the problems of economic insecurity and social injustice.

Some anarchists, like Bakunin, believed that change would come only through the violent uprising of the masses and fighting in the barricades. The German anarchist John Most, who came to the United States during the labor ferment of the 1880's, also believed in violent revolution. But the greatest and most profound anarchist thinker, Peter Kropotkin, a Russian prince who gave up his royal title in order to join the anarchist movement, rejected violence. He saw the State itself as an agency of violence, an instrument of force and oppression; he believed that only through cooperation and mutual aid could man attain freedom—socially, economically, politically. Though the dissenters in this book were not part of the political anarchist movement, most of them defended the right of such radical dissent.

The lives of these six dissenters intertwined, and to some extent they were influenced by one another. Both Eugene V. Debs and Clarence Darrow idolized Robert Ingersoll who was orthodox in politics but unorthodox in religion. Ingersoll, the Republican, toured the State of Illinois in opposition to Altgeld the Democrat, yet he later supported the governor's controversial action in the Haymarket affair. Although Darrow worked with Jane Addams, he looked upon her as a reformer who wanted to put salve on the wounds of society while he considered himself a radical who wished to go to the roots of the causes of poverty. Darrow loved Debs and respected Lincoln Steffens. Steffens, who was Darrow's friend, knew the politically strong and their weaknesses, and he muckraked their corruption. Debs, who sought Darrow's legal advice in 1894 in support of a labor cause, did not want his services when he was charged with opposing the government's war efforts in 1917 because Darrow supported that war. With the exception of Steffens, all of these dissenters were either born or raised in the Midwest. Chance brought Steffens to Chicago, where he started his muckraking career.

Why are their voices relevant?

Always the Challenge

Dissent has always been an integral part of the American scene. Though there were many whose contributions to protest were as important—or sometimes more important—the individuals in this book were selected because each represents a distinct form of dissent. They worked in law, in theology, in social work and politics, in journalism and the labor movement. All acted on principle, unafraid of any consequences to themselves. They were not nihilists; they desired to build: in place of social and economic inequality, they demanded the dignity of all people; instead of accepted political, economic, and religious tenets, they urged, and even demanded, intellectual scrutiny; instead of superstition they pleaded for reason; and instead of war, international order with a view toward world peace and stability. They insisted, moreover, that any opinion has a right to be heard.

Their lives are relevant because many of the issues they faced are similar to those of today's dissenters. Debs went to jail because he opposed World War I; one of Darrow's main concerns was the plight of the underprivileged, the black man in particular; Jane Addams withstood the wrath of the Establishment as she talked peace during war; Ingersoll questioned religious orthodoxy, which did not permit free investigation; Altgeld sacrificed his political career to see justice accomplished in the Haymarket affair; Steffens never ceased to question the established order as he exposed the corruption and immorality of its institutions.

Their lives are relevant today—as they always will be—because of their courage, their uncompromising defense of dissent, their individualism, and their integrity.

Lincoln Steffens

Courtesy of The New-York Historical Society, New York City

LINCOLN STEFFENS
1866-1936
Muckraker and Journalist

WHEN LINCOLN STEFFENS was a defense witness on behalf of his friend Clarence Darrow in 1912, the prosecuting attorney asked him if he was an anarchist. Steffens replied that he was a good deal worse, that he believed in Christianity. "Anarchism, you understand, merely believes in justice," he said. "Christianity is a doctrine, what they call love, which I interpret to be understanding mercy, and I don't believe that justice is what we want. I believe we have got to have more of a personal feeling; more mercy, and more understanding."

There was no hate in Steffens as he lectured the prosecution, no self-righteousness. His eyes and his voice were soft, compassionate. His appearance—slim figure, goatee, string tie, eyeglasses—suggested an artist, a philosophical seeker of the truth rather than a militant muckraker.

But Steffens did not feel hate or self-righteousness even when he muckraked the cities, states, and big business of the United States. What he always looked for was the *cause* of corruption—and he found it, not in people but in circumstances. As long as the economic system was based on privilege, Steffens believed, it made no difference whether the government and the industries were controlled by the good people or the bad. The system created the morality, and nothing would change as long as the system continued to exist.

He tried to explain this during a meeting on the West Coast when a minister asked him who had founded the system of evil. Steffens insisted that the real evil was the policy of privileges. He continued, "Most people put the blame on Adam. Adam says no, he was not to blame, it was Eve, the woman. Eve insists it wasn't she, it was the serpent.

"But I am here trying to show you that it was, it is, the apple."

Steffens desired to help people explain themselves. He had the ability to get them to confide in him, to tell him the truth as they saw it. Yet he was always searching for more, never believing he had found all the truth. "Life is a struggle," he would say, "between two sides who don't understand each other—both are right, both are wrong."

Lincoln Steffens was raised in Sacramento, California, by parents who from the beginning encouraged their son to explore, to examine, to understand the world around him. His father, Joseph Steffens, was the son of a pioneer farmer from eastern Canada who had migrated to Illinois where he preached, farmed, bred cattle, and raced and bet on horses. Because Joseph was small and weak and not suited to the physically demanding farm work, he left Illinois as a young man and went to San Francisco where he became a bookkeeper in a large paint, oil, and glass company. He met his wife, Elizabeth Louisa Symes, an English girl, at the boardinghouse where they both roomed. She had traveled from New York to San Francisco in the early 1860's by way of the Isthmus of Panama for the specific purpose of finding a husband.

They had four children, of whom Joseph Lincoln Steffens was the eldest and the only son, born in San Francisco on April 6, 1866. When he and his three sisters were still very young, the family moved to Sacramento where the father, now a partner in the company for which he worked, managed its Sacramento store. He had a prospering business, and the Steffens family lived comfortably in one of the city's largest homes, which later became the executive mansion of the governor of California.

The young Steffens found little to interest him in school. He would much rather have been wandering through the countryside than spending his time in the schoolroom. He was almost always at the bottom of his class in grammar school, where he failed his last year. As a result, his father sent him to a military school in San Mateo. The military school discipline, however, neither subdued the boy nor turned him into a conforming student. Just learning the facts was never enough for him; he needed to know the reasons why, and he questioned the implications of everything he heard and read. He found that people spoke in absolutes—things were all good or all bad—but when he asked questions, nobody could answer to his satisfaction, not even his teachers.

In his first attempt to enter the University of California he failed his entrance examinations. His father enrolled him in a private school and hired a tutor who not only inspired scholarship but gave the boy direction in his seeking, taught him how to question constructively. When Steffens took his entrance examinations the second time, he was admitted to the University at Berkeley, and from there he received his Bachelor of Philosophy degree at the age of twenty-three. The most important truth he learned at the California institution was that "nothing is done. Nothing is known. Everything in the world remains to be done or done over."

Steffens, still seeking answers, was determined to further his education abroad. "Rebel though I was, I had got the religion of scholarship and science; I was in awe of the authorities in the academic world," he explained in his autobiography as he described this period of his life.

He spent three years at German universities and in Paris and England. To the young student, Germany in the summer of 1889 meant not only university study but cafés, music halls, and art. In Berlin, Steffens visited the famous galleries. At Heidelberg, he studied under Kuno Fischer and heard him lecture on Hegel's philosophy; in Leipzig he listened to Wilhelm Wundt discuss his theories of experimental psychology. He was left confused and dissatisfied, convinced that there was no science of ethics in either philosophy or psychology.

Sitting behind Steffens in Wundt's lectures was Josephine Bontecou, an American psychology student ten years older than he. They fell in love and left Germany together. After traveling through the Alps, they lived in the Latin Quarter in Paris and studied at the Sorbonne. There Steffens, particularly, attended numerous lectures, always in search of the meaning of life as it related to people's actions; in London they studied at the British Museum. Writing to his mother about Josephine, Steffens professed that "my love for Josephine has only made all the love I ever bore anyone burn all the warmer and brighter, for she is a noble, earnest little woman, and calls out all that is best in me."

They were married secretly in October 1891 and returned to the United States a year later. Steffens planned to teach in California, and he assumed his father would continue to help him financially until he was earning enough. Joseph, however, not knowing of the marriage, decided it was time his twenty-six-year-old son was self-supporting. The young married couple were shocked to find a letter awaiting them in New York from Steffens's father which said, "By now you must know about all there is to know of the theory of life, but there's a practical side as well. It's worth knowing. I suggest that you learn it, and the way to study it, I think, is to stay in New York and hustle." One hundred dollars was enclosed with the letter to keep Steffens until he could find a job and support himself.

Lincoln Steffens and his wife decided to remain in New York. He tried short-story writing, but after his first piece, which he sold to *Harper's Weekly*, he had difficulty selling any more. He looked for work—any kind of work. Although there were many want ads for jobs on the New York waterfront, he had difficulty getting hired. "Next to my London clothes and general beautifulness, the heaviest handicap I had was my claim to a college education, and not only one college, but—five," he recalled drolly many years later.

Eventually, he used a letter of introduction his father obtained for him. It led to his first job on the New York *Evening Post* where he did general reporting, from writing about a missing stockbroker to interviewing the superintendent of schools.

Steffens had a "nose" for news; he was curious, persistent, and determined, and he inspired trust and confidence. With his remarkable insight and analytic powers, he had the ability to get the most out of an interview. His own interest in the nature of good and bad, in who and what, in how and why, helped to make him an excellent investigative reporter. After several months, the *Evening Post* assigned him to Wall Street where he met the leaders of industry and commerce. They agreed to exchange confidences: each would do his own research and investigation; the bankers would then share their information with Steffens before it became public knowledge, and he in turn would let them know of the rumors and reports he heard on Wall Street before they were published in his newspaper. Each association became for Steffens research into the morals of the times, into the corruption and graft which were affecting the nation.

In his next major assignment, Steffens followed the activities of the Reverend Dr. Charles Parkhurst, the crusader who was waging a war against police corruption. From his pulpit at the Madison Square Presbyterian Church, Dr. Parkhurst exposed a relationship between the New York police and Tammany Hall, the center of political power in the city, and between the liquor interests and the criminals. Steffens made a working pact with the minister, similar to the one he had had on Wall Street with the bankers and brokers: both he and Dr. Parkhurst would conduct their own investigations and then exchange their findings, thus getting a broader understanding of all the facts involved.

In this new assignment, Steffens worked out of police headquarters in a tenement neighborhood. This meant also reporting police news, politics, strikes, and the activities of the Jewish Lower East Side ghetto with its synagogues and theaters. While gathering news about a fire in one synagogue, Steffens was inspired to attend a service in another. He felt drawn to the ancient traditions and customs, and, in his own words, he became "almost a Jew," attending services on the Jewish holidays and fasting on Yom Kippur, the Jewish Day of Atonement. He even had a *mezuzah*

—a small tube containing passages from the Torah, a part of the Old Testament—nailed to his office door. In the ghetto, also, Steffens watched strikers clashing with scabs, those workers who cross the picket lines, and he saw police clubbing the strikers. The brutality outraged him.

During this period the Lexow Committee, investigating crime in New York, disclosed a graft ring in the police department. Steffens became interested in Captain Max Schmittberger, who had confessed his part in the system of police corruption. Schmittberger told how he collected "payoffs" during his early days as a policeman in the Tenderloin district, an area dominated by hotels, theaters, saloons, gambling houses, and houses of prostitution. As a captain of the district he supervised the collection and distribution of the "protection" money to the policemen in the area and to the inspector of the district.

"Can an honest man do dishonest things and remain honest?" Steffens asked as he first helped to expose Schmittberger and then encouraged the police captain to eliminate bribery and corruption from his precinct.

Steffens answered his own question, "Yes," for the former police captain, given another chance, eventually became chief of police of New York City, where he served with honesty and efficiency.

The Lexow police exposure initiated a reform wave which led to the defeat of Tammany Hall. The new reform mayor appointed the dynamic, flamboyant, and ambitious Theodore Roosevelt as police commissioner, the first step in Roosevelt's political climb to the Presidency of the United States.

About this time, Steffens received a cable from the German consulate at Naples. Johann Friedrich Krudewolf, a German friend from his student days in Europe, had died and left him an estate of twelve thousand dollars.

"Money is freedom," Krudewolf had often told Lincoln Steffens—and freedom was what his inheritance came to mean to Steffens. The Panic of 1893 had made a deep impression on the young reporter as he covered the Wall Street scene. The uncertainty of America's economy and the undependability, even unpredictability, of the American business leaders had affected him deeply. With lessons from his Wall Street reporting days, Steffens skillfully speculated with half his inheritance. His father borrowed the other half—to hold for him. Steffens's investment grew. Slowly, he made enough money to be financially secure. Without dependence on a job, the young truth seeker was able to go wherever his questions led.

In 1897 Steffens left the *Evening Post* to become city editor of the failing *Commercial Advertiser*, where he made it a policy to hire writers instead of experienced reporters. He told them to write with enthusiasm, to feel and to make the readers feel the life of the city: rich and poor, ugly and beautiful, the happiness and the tragedy. The only way he wanted to beat competition was in the way a story was written.

The reporting of a murder, he insisted, should be told in such a way that the murderer would not be hanged, at least not by readers of the *Commercial Advertiser*. "If you get so used to police news that a murder is not a human tragedy but only a crime," Steffens warned his writers, "you can't write police news for us."

Within four years Steffens and his associates had made the *Advertiser* an exciting newspaper; but he felt the need for a new challenge, and when he was offered the job of managing editor on *McClure's Magazine*, he accepted. In affiliating with *McClure's*, Lincoln Steffens became part of a publishing revolution started in the early 1890's when low-priced magazines were made possible by new printing and engraving processes. These new publications were generally well edited, lively in both content and format, and popular with the public.

Several months after Steffens joined the magazine, the perceptive S. S. McClure, its publisher, decided that his managing editor needed to familiarize himself with the country. He suggested that Steffens go to *McClure's* advertising department, learn where they had railroad credit, get a ticket, and go—anywhere. The magazine had a bill against the Lackawanna Railroad, which went to Chicago, and in that city Steffens made the first contacts which led to his muckraking career.

McClure had told his editor to seek out new writing talents, learn what leading citizens were interested in reading, and find ideas for new articles. A Chicago lawyer whom Steffens visited suggested that he go to Minneapolis and talk with a man by the name of Weyerhauser, one of the richest men in the country, owner of timberlands in the West and Northwest. With the understanding that what he said be kept confidential, Weyerhauser told Steffens how he used politics to amass his land: how he had made contributions to campaign funds, first to influence the local politicians, later to affect court decisions. This was a big story, but Steffens could not use it because of his agreement with Weyerhauser that their conversations be off the record. It gave him, however, invaluable insight for future stories.

The lawyer who had sent Steffens to Weyerhauser next advised him to see Joseph W. Folk, crusading circuit attorney of St. Louis. Folk welcomed Steffens and related how leading businessmen made deals to get franchises, licenses, exemptions, and grants. The newspapers were encouraging Folk in his investigations, some enthusiastically printing the news he gave them. Nevertheless, Folk feared that once the publishers learned the ramifications of his exposures he would lose all local support. He urged Steffens, who was not subject to the same pressures as the St. Louis press, to publish the results of his investigations.

Steffens commissioned Claude H. Wetmore, a St. Louis newspaperman, to write the story, but when the article was submitted some important facts had been omitted. Wetmore argued that if these were included he could not continue to live or work in St. Louis. He insisted that, if the full truth had to be reported, Steffens's name, too, must appear on the article. In this way, he said, he could always blame his coauthor.

"Tweed Days in St. Louis" by Wetmore and Steffens appeared in the October 1902 issue of *McClure's Magazine*. Folk, as a result of the disclosures, was not reelected circuit attorney, but the national publicity he received throughout the state was so favorable that he was later elected governor of Missouri.

In his long discussions with Folk and through his own investigations, Steffens began to evolve the theory which he continued to believe the rest of his life—an idea first suggested to him by Folk. Bribery was not mere felony, Steffens decided. It was a revolutionary process going on in all cities. If he could trace it to its source, he thought, he could find the cause of political corruption—and its cure.

He visited and he studied other cities—among them Minneapolis, New York, Pittsburgh, Philadelphia. In all of them, large and small, he found that every department of government was affected, that graft touched each one, that many respectable citizens gained special privileges as a result of the corruption. For every bribe taker there was a bribe giver. Privilege, not men, caused evil.

Steffens's second article, "The Shame of Minneapolis," carrying only his byline, appeared in the January 1903 issue of *McClure's Magazine*. The same issue contained Ray Stannard Baker's "The Right to Work" and another installment of Ida Tarbell's "History of Standard Oil." All had the same theme—citizens either breaking the law or letting it be broken. Baker's article showed how unions kept nonunion men from working; Ida Tarbell pointed to capitalists conspiring among themselves to break the law where it restrained them and to enforce the law to hold back others who stood in their way.

That these three articles appeared in the same issue was pure accident. "We did not plan it so," explained an editorial by S. S. McClure. "It is a coincidence that the January *McClure's* is such an arraignment of American character as should make every one of us stop and think." These articles cited the universality of the dangerous trait of corruption in American life, McClure wrote. "Capitalists, workingmen, politicians, citizens—all breaking the law, or letting it be broken. Who is left to uphold it? The lawyers? Some of the best lawyers in this country are hired, not to go into court to defend cases, but to advise corporations and business firms how they can get around the law without too great a risk of punishment. The judges? Too many of them so respect the laws that for some 'error' or quibble they restore to office and liberty men convicted on evidence overwhelmingly convincing to common sense. The churches? We know of one, an ancient and wealthy establishment, which had to be compelled by a Tammany hold-over health officer to put its tenements in sanitary condition. The colleges? They do not understand.

"There is no one left; none but all of us. . . . We all are doing our worst and making the public pay. The public is the people. We forget that we all are the people; that while each of us in his group can shove off on the rest the bill of today, the debt is only postponed; the rest are passing it on back to us. We have to pay in the end, every one of us. And in the end the sum total of the debt will be our liberty."

The muckraking era had begun. Exposure became the national vogue. Corruption was found in every quarter, with a widespread breaking of the law. No cures were offered, but the sins were detailed as such magazines as *Collier's, Cosmopolitan, Hampton's, Everybody's, American Magazine,* and *Independent* became vehicles for exposure. A new school of writers and editors came on the scene who gave realistic accounts of what they saw as the true character of American life. Upton Sinclair described the filth in the Chicago stockyards in his novel *The Jungle,* and Samuel Hopkins Adams unmasked the fraudulent claims and endorsements of patent medicines in *The Great American Fraud;* both were important to the passage of the Pure Food and Drug Act. Thomas Lawson wrote about the stock market in *Frenzied Finance,* a series of articles which played a large part in welding public opinion for government regulation of the stock market and culminated in the Senate Pujo Committee investigation in 1913; many of the safeguards Lawson demanded were put into effect through the Securities Act of 1933. Mark Sullivan was among the first to disclose the autocratic power of the Speaker of the

United States House of Representatives, Joseph G. Cannon, and his writings were largely responsible for the eventual defeat of Cannon as Speaker.

Steffens's articles about the various cities were collected in his first book, *The Shame of the Cities*, which continues to be used as a reference work on the process of political corruption. In a clear and sophisticated writing style, he presented the issues objectively and factually to a receptive public. He dedicated the book "to the accused—to all the citizens of all the cities in the United States," laying the responsibility for the ugly state of affairs directly on the shoulders of his own readers.

Steffens's exposure of political bosses and cities was followed by a study of the state administrations of Missouri, Illinois, Wisconsin, Rhode Island, Ohio, and New Jersey. Here, too, with the exception of Robert M. La Follette's Wisconsin, Steffens found that the "system" cooperated with graft. The bribers and the bribed, the corruptionists and the corrupted, were all intertwined and bound by special privilege.

La Follette, governor of Wisconsin at the turn of the nineteenth century, later senator from that state, was one of Steffens's heroes. Originally, Steffens was challenged to go into Wisconsin and investigate the La Follette machine, but after careful investigation he decided that La Follette "was restoring representative government" in Wisconsin "by his oratory and his fierce dictatorship" and his "relentless conspicuous persistence."

Steffens's articles on the states were published as his

second book, *The Struggle for Self-Government,* with a satirical dedication to the Czar of Russia whose subjects were starting to demand representation: "Your Majesty seems to wish to rule, you alone. Your people are demanding representation in your government. Apparently you both regard your purposes as cross and incompatible. They are not so. Read my book and you will see that we Americans have what we call 'representative democracy'; but we have Czars, too. It's true we do not call them by that title; we call them bosses. But names and titles, like forms and charters, are intended to deceive men, not the rulers of men, and our bosses are autocrats, Sire, as you are; no more so, but no less."

Despite this cynicism Steffens felt that there was hope. It lay in a new kind of leadership. In his next book, *Upbuilders,* he portrayed reform leaders such as Judge Benjamin B. Lindsey, a county judge in Denver, who established one of the first juvenile courts in the United States; Rudolph Spreckels, a California businessman, who led a campaign to expose political corruption in his state; W. S. U'Ren, a political lobbyist in Oregon and father of the initiative and referendum, who built a reform machine and fought the lumber and railroad interests; and Everett Colby, a rich man's son, who led a reform movement in New Jersey. Steffens asserted that the people would follow "a leader who was loyal to them, brave, and not too far ahead," and then "the solution of our common problems; the problems of the cities, states and nations

—the problem of civilized living in human communities"—could begin.

Who was the first muckraker? Ray Stannard Baker, Mark Sullivan, and Lincoln Steffens all claimed the distinction. Ida Tarbell was chagrined to find herself included with the muckrakers and later turned to writing eulogies of business. Historians generally concede the title to Steffens, who himself was so sure he deserved it that in his autobiography he captioned a photograph of a page from "Tweed Days in St. Louis" as "The first muckraking article."

The writers and editors of the reform movement of the early 1900's were encouraged by President Theodore Roosevelt, the former New York reform police chief of Steffens's early reporting days, who acted on many of the evils being exposed. The President frequently invited a writer or his editor to lunch at the White House as his way of saying thank you for the exposures.

These reformers were soon to learn, however, that the President was not always fully in accord with their writings, particularly when they attacked his friends. They first became aware of the President's feelings when *Cosmopolitan* began to publish a series of articles called "The Treason of the Senate," written by David Graham Phillips. In announcing the series, the magazine proclaimed that the title was "fit and logical" for "this terrible arraignment of those who, sitting in the seats of the mighty at Washington, have betrayed the public to that cruel and vicious Spirit of Mammon which has come to dominate the nation."

The first at whom this charge was leveled was New York Senator Chauncey Depew. Phillips accused him of being in the pay of "the interests" as a member of the boards of directors of seventy corporations and receiving more than $50,000 in fees from these firms for services rendered. This was the same Depew of whom John Peter Altgeld, governor of Illinois, had once said, "Go thou and do evil that thou mayest live on the fat of the land, and that thy sleekness may be the wonder of men."

When the *Cosmopolitan* article on Depew appeared, President Roosevelt, a friend of the senator, reacted immediately in a sentimental defense of him. He showed his displeasure first in an off-the-record speech before the Washington, D. C., Gridiron Club, in March 1906. A month later he repeated the same speech at dedication ceremonies of the cornerstone of the new building of the House of Representatives.

Roosevelt compared these writers who were exposing corruption to the man with the muckrake in John Bunyan's *Pilgrim's Progress,* who could "look no way but downward, with a muckrake in his hands." Even though he was "offered a celestial crown" he could "neither look up nor regard the crown he was offered." All he could do was "rake to himself the filth of the floor," President Roosevelt said as he muckraked the muckrakers.

Steffens, visiting President Roosevelt at the White

House the day after the speech, accused him of having put an end to the very process of journalistic exposure that had helped to propel him into the Presidency. But Roosevelt replied that he had not meant Steffens or some of the others. "It was that article on poor old Chauncey Depew." He said he had spoken to comfort Depew.

That same year, 1906, Steffens, Ray Stannard Baker, and Ida Tarbell resigned from *McClure's* and joined with Finley Peter Dunne, creator of the famous political commentary of "Mr. Dooley," and with William Allen White, writer and editor, in publishing the *American Magazine.*

Steffens remained with the *American* for only a short time. He left when he realized that the prospect of earning more money for the magazine caused him to be less objective in his writing, and he determined never to work where he had money invested. For a while he was associated with *Everybody's Magazine,* which continued investigative reporting. During this time he went to Harvard University to seek from its graduating class "the ablest mind that could express itself in writing." There he found the now famous political commentator Walter Lippmann, whom he hired to work for *Everybody's.*

Steffens turned to free-lance writing as he became convinced that exposure alone was not the answer to corruption and injustice. Something more was necessary. Man needed vision, hope, an ideal. Where could these be found? he asked himself.

He studied socialism, and he studied the theory of Single Tax, a doctrine propounded by Henry George, that government tax only the value of land and abolish all other types of taxes. Neither had the answer for him. More and more he turned to the social ideas of Christianity. He read and reread the New Testament and found solace in it. He attended church services in the cities he visited, yet he felt he "never heard Christianity, as Jesus taught it in the New Testament, preached to the Christians." But Christianity, Steffens concluded, "unpreached and untaught and unlearned among the righteous, works wonders still among the sinners."

This was the mood of the forty-five-year-old Steffens when he learned about the bombing of the Los Angeles *Times* building and the subsequent arrests of two active union men, the McNamara brothers, who were charged with the dynamiting. Steffens decided the case provided an opportunity to "test" Christianity. Since he knew that labor in many instances used violence, he believed the McNamara brothers, as part of organized labor, were indeed guilty of the violent act with which they were charged.

Steffens arranged to report the trial for a group of newspapers, not to write about the procedures of the case but to discuss the *cause* of the act. A trial judge, he insisted, could not mete out justice in such a case because he would permit evidence only as it related to the murder charge. This was not enough for Steffens. He wanted to know why, despite labor's cry of a frame-up, a conservative labor union found it necessary to use dynamite in its struggle against the employer. Steffens felt that the use of violence as in the McNamara case was a "social crime in social warfare" and that the real cause lay in economics and psychology, that conventional moral judgments of right and wrong could not be applied in labor war.

Los Angeles was an open-shop city in which there was little or no union organization. The Los Angeles *Times* led the anti-union forces in using strong-arm tactics to fight labor organization. Since San Francisco, five hundred miles to the north, was a strong union city with high wages, industry began to move from there, with many of the companies going to Los Angeles. To equalize wages and to keep industry from moving to Los Angeles and other nonunion cities, San Francisco labor men started to organize Los Angeles.

"If the San Francisco gorillas succeed," fumed General Harrison Gray Otis, publisher of the Los Angeles *Times*, "then the brilliant future of Los Angeles will end, business will stagnate; Los Angeles will be another San Francisco—dead."

The scene was set for confrontation.

On the morning of October 1, 1910, after the editorial staff had left the *Times*'s offices and the next day's edition was being printed, an explosion shattered the rear of the building. Fire followed; twenty people were killed and many injured.

Otis editorialized, "O you anarchic scum, you cowardly murderers . . . you midnight assassins."

Eugene Victor Debs, however, the labor agitator and

Socialist, wrote in the October 15, 1910, *Appeal to Reason,* "I want to express my deliberate opinion that the *Times* and its crowd of union-haters are the instigators, if not the actual perpetrators, of that crime."

Six months later, on April 23, 1911, the *Times* carried a page-one story with the headline:

DYNAMITERS OF THE TIMES BUILDING CAUGHT
CRIME TRACED DIRECTLY TO HIGH UNION OFFICIALS
RED-HANDED UNION CHIEFS IMPLICATED IN CONSPIRACY

Samuel Gompers, president of the American Federation of Labor, retorted, "The whole affair smacks of well-laid prearrangements."

Labor raised a fund to defend John J. McNamara, secretary-treasurer of the International Association of Bridge and Structural Workers of the American Federation of Labor, and James B. McNamara, his brother. The unions hired labor's friend, Clarence Darrow, to defend the men (see Darrow, pp. 104 ff.).

Darrow and his associates were struggling to complete the jury selection when Steffens arrived in Los Angeles. He sensed Darrow's doubts concerning the innocence of his clients and proposed to attempt a compromise with the prosecution. Though skeptical, Darrow agreed to Steffens's suggestion, but with the understanding that the defense not be identified as having initiated such a move. Steffens contended that all the parties involved were sinners, and "Christianity does work with sinners. . . . Political bosses and business bosses, out-and-out crooks, hardboiled editors, roughneck rascals—they never failed to respond to the (unnamed) Christian appeal, especially for mercy." He talked with state officials, businessmen, labor leaders, and the McNamara brothers, to convince them to negotiate an agreement in which the brothers would plead guilty and serve specific prison terms. In turn, the state would agree not to prosecute any other union members connected with the case, and both labor and management would meet to settle their differences.

Even in a time much less complex than today, there is a disarming innocence in Steffens's idea of compromise as a way "to try out Christianity as a working principle" and put the "Golden Rule" into effect in its simplest and most elemental form—"All things whatsoever ye would that men should do to you, do ye even so to them."

Although Steffens believed he had been successful in his compromise negotiations, his sentimental experiment failed. The terms of the sentences initially settled upon were increased, two additional labor men were eventually convicted and sent to the penitentiary, there was no labor-management conference, and, as an aftermath, Clarence Darrow, the defense attorney, was indicted on charges of attempting to bribe a juror. Years later, when Steffens again pleaded for clemency for the men still serving jail sentences, he once more failed.

As a witness for Darrow in the case of the defense attorney versus the State of California, Steffens tried to answer the question of why social crimes are committed.

The prosecutor asked him, "You don't see anything wrong in attempting to get a man free from punishment whom you know to be guilty of a crime against the state, do you, Mr. Steffens?"

"No," Lincoln Steffens answered. "Not if that crime is not an individual crime, but what I would call a social crime, a crime that is a result of the feelings of a large part of a people of resentment against certain conditions that I would call more a revolutionary crime, and not a . . . legal crime."

"And you believe that such a crime was the crime of a warfare?"

"Yes."

The prosecutor continued this theme, asking, "All right, and you believe you were justified in going to any length to protect such men as they were, such as you found them to be, from punishment, under those circumstances?"

"I believed," Steffens answered firmly, "that I was right to go to the length that I did go, which was to appeal to the reason of all these men. Now, your question might have left me, if I had answered carelessly, as admitting that I would consent to murder. . . . I would not do that."

The prosecutor asked, "You would believe that it would be perfectly justifiable under the circumstances of warfare, which you believed to exist, Mr. Steffens, if necessary to save those men, you believe it would be justifiable even to bribe jurors?"

"No. My feeling about bribery is exactly like my feeling about murder or the bribery of legislators, or any other force. . . . I think these crimes are not justifiable, but I think they are understandable . . . our legal machinery and our system of punishments cannot and should not be used to solve social problems. That when a big case like this McNamara case comes up under the form of law, as a mere murder case, it is all right to send J. B. McNamara to jail; it is even all right to send J. J. McNamara to jail, but we must not think when we have sent those two individuals away, that we have solved the problem that produced them."

The failure of the Los Angeles experiment in the McNamara case almost convinced Steffens that the Golden Rule and the force of goodwill might not be strong enough to bring out the best in man. Although disillusioned, he continued to defend his compromise experiment before hostile labor audiences in debates and lectures, and he looked for opportunities to try it again. For a long time after the trial he continued to be derisively called "Golden Rule" Steffens by both labor and capital.

During the next few years, Steffens continued to write about free speech, strikes, the unemployed, and to use whatever influence he had to help these causes; he also worked on a book on Boston which was never published. Steffens theorized that free speech can be a defense against mob action. In the early 1900's in New York's Union Square, a group of anarchists was meeting to protest police indignities. Eager to prove his theory, Steffens persuaded the chief of police to permit the speakers to talk without police interference. If the police would not react to the agitation, he reasoned, there would be no trouble. He was right: the orators spoke, decrying the police, the system; the crowd listened and then dispersed.

When World War I broke out in 1914, Steffens was in Europe studying politics and governments. The war forced him to change his plans, and he went to Mexico, which was in the midst of a revolution. Wanting to learn more about it, he joined with Venustiano Carranza, one of the two Mexican revolutionary leaders, and traveled with him throughout the country. For the next few years, Steffens devoted his time and energies to interpreting the Mexican events to the American people and remonstrating against the attempts of interventionists to crush the revolution which, he asserted, was neither caused nor started by radicals. The leaders of the movement wanted reform, he insisted, but the Mexican Establishment was so corrupt that, at the first push of the forces unleashed by the reform, the government collapsed.

The opportunity to see a second revolution was given to him by his friend Charles R. Crane, industrialist and diplomat, who invited Steffens to go with him to Russia. Within six days, Steffens was sailing with Crane for Bergen, Norway, where they boarded a train for Petrograd, now Leningrad. The Crane party, on a diplomatic mission, was one of the first delegations from a foreign country to enter Russia after the overthrow of the Czar. Here again Steffens believed he had found proof that revolutionists did not cause rebellions. The Russian revolution, he observed, dethroned the Czar because of the corruption and ineptitude of the government.

After he came back to the United States, Steffens traveled the country—from New York to Los Angeles—explaining, sympathetically, both the Russian and the Mexican revolutions to his American audiences.

He visited Eugene Victor Debs, who was serving a prison sentence for opposing World War I (see Debs, pp. 80 ff.). "Tell me all about the Russian Revolution," Debs asked. "Is it true about the violence, the horror, the terror, the tyranny, the bloodshed which the Bolsheviks are effecting?"

"It's all true, Gene. But you must remember that a revolution is no gentleman."

In the spring of 1919 Steffens returned to Russia, this time as a member of the semiofficial Bullitt peace mission representing the United States. In Russia, William C. Bullitt arranged for Steffens to interview Lenin and other Bolsheviks. Russia is a "most absolute dictatorship," Steffens reported. He explained that its leaders knew it and were unhappy about it but they felt this would change once the goals of the economic revolution were attained. The Bolsheviks seek to remove the causes of poverty, graft, corruption, war, privilege, Steffens said, insisting, "I have seen the future. And it works!"

Although he remained sympathetic to the Bolshevik regime, he never became a member of the Communist party. He could write, "I am a patriot for Russia; the Future is there; Russia will win out and will save the world." But he could also say, "I don't want to live there. It is too much like serving in an army at war with no mercy for the weak and no time for the wounded."

On his way home from Russia the journalist visited Paris. Here, Steffens, a widower for the previous eight years, met and fell in love with Ella Winter, a young English economics student, whom he described as "one of the happiest things I had ever seen. . . . This girl danced, her eyes danced, her mind, her hands, her feet danced as she ran" about her errands in Paris where she had been assigned to an American peace group by the London School of Economics. She was too young, Steffens told himself, and he smothered his feeling for her by likening her to a boy and calling her Peter. Peter followed him to Italy when he interviewed Mussolini.

Steffens was impressed with the Italian dictator, whom he saw as a new kind of political boss. It was a peculiar weakness of Lincoln Steffens that he was fascinated by strong men, whether captains of industry or labor leaders or dictators of the Left like Lenin and of the Right like Mussolini. He had a naïve inability to view them realistically.

The age difference between Steffens and Ella Winter—more than thirty years—worried Steffens. But he could not put her out of his mind, and he stopped trying to do so when he learned that she was also in love with him. Four years after they met they were married in Italy. A year later, at the age of fifty-nine, Steffens became a father for the first and only time. He was the proudest of fathers, devoting himself in the early years almost exclusively to his small son. He delighted in the little boy's development and wrote charming letters to Ella's mother detailing the progress of her young grandson. Becoming a father in his "dotage," as he described it, was a miracle of life to Steffens and filled him with humility and gratitude.

Until 1926 the family lived in Italy where Steffens wrote *Moses in Red* and started his autobiography. *Moses in Red* was Steffens' interpretation of the revolt of Israel from Egyptian slavery, which he saw as a typical revolution. In this book he proposed that "in revolutions, in wars and in all such disorganizing, free-spreading crises in human affairs, nations tend to return to the first, the simplest and perhaps the best form of government: a dictatorship." He believed dictatorships are a natural development when people grow frightened by economic and political crises. Then they look for a leader, and they follow compliantly. Steffens saw this happen in both Russia and Italy. He thought he understood Mussolini's observation "that there is an empty throne in every country and that, given the emergency, the bold men can seize it—and hold it." Steffens never blamed such leaders as Lenin and Mussolini, or the political bosses who dominated the American scene, for the evils they helped to perpetrate against society. He blamed the weakness of those people who let themselves be captured and held powerless.

He believed in freedom, too, but as man's last achievement, and only achieved when society has as its base an "unprivileged system of economics." Not political action but only a revolution could bring this about, he claimed.

The Autobiography of Lincoln Steffens, published in 1931 in two volumes, is a panorama of people, places, and events, of politicians and poets, lawyers and writers, dictators and anarchists, preachers and policemen, of revolution and counterrevolution, crime waves and reform, magazines and newspapers. Steffens's power to reminisce, his ability to see himself in a humorous light, his probing of social problems, his talent as a writer, and his receptiveness to new ideas and methods made the book a best seller almost immediately. It brought political excitement to the college campuses as it portrayed Steffens's disenchantment with the Establishment and his evolvement from a muckraker to an apologist for the Soviet Union, from a reformer and progressive to a revolutionist. His *Autobiography* reflects a kinship with much of the student rebellion on college campuses today. For Steffens, too, found much to criticize in this area. As early as 1923 he wrote to his sister, "Damn these universities, all of them. They have made my life one of unlearning literally, and all my discoveries are of well-known, well-kept secrets."

Brought once more to national prominence by his book, Steffens began to write a column for three local California periodicals in which he discussed things, people, and events that interested him. Sometimes pessimistic, sometimes with an air of optimism, he jabbed at "rugged individualism" and "special privilege," always with the sense of humor he felt was necessary to life.

Two years after the publication of his autobiography, Steffens became ill while on a lecture tour and returned to his home in Carmel, California, "The Gateway," which became a mecca for visitors coming to talk with America's foremost muckraker.

An ailing Steffens continued to write for the three California journals. One of his last columns was about Spain, inflamed by civil war. Spain, where the forces of fascism and Nazism first battled freedom, was the training ground for World War II. "Spain is the first, the opening battle of man for man; perhaps it is the most decisive battle. Anyway it is ours, as they must know and we must. I say we do, and that we realize as they fight that we have to finish what they are starting. The Spanish defenders are our world's leaders," he wrote.

Steffens was collecting some of these columns for

book publication when he died on August 9, 1936. He had already written an introduction to the volume, *Steffens Speaking* (published posthumously): "When I finished my life, I did not die as I might gracefully have done. I lived on and, of course, I learned and unlearned as always."

Two years after his death the letters of Lincoln Steffens were published revealing a more personal and human side of the muckraker: his relationships to family and friends, to the woman who had been his mistress both before his marriage to Josephine Bontecou and after her death, his depth of feeling for his young wife Ella Winter and their son, are remarkably portrayed in these letters spanning almost two-thirds of his life.

"Learning and unlearning," Steffens, as a fearless journalist and social critic, exposed political corruption to the public gaze, all the while searching more for the causes of the evils than for the wrongs themselves. No one was immune to corruption, he was saddened to learn. Reform failed, since even the reformer could be bought by the system of special privilege. The system itself had to be abolished, Steffens finally decided, and although he would not become a member of the Communist party, he felt that within its philosophy lay the destruction of corruption. A questioner who could laugh at himself, Steffens remains a force for constructive dissent at a time when dissent and rebellion are in the forefront of contemporary life.

Lincoln Steffens

Thirty-one years after Steffen's death, Sigma Delta Chi, the professional journalism fraternity, marked "The Gateway" with a plaque as a:

Historic Site in Journalism
Honoring the Memory of
Lincoln Steffens
1866–1936

Here in "The Gateway" the greatest
of the journalistic crusaders known as "Muckrakers"
passed the later years of a full and vibrant life

Eugene Victor Debs

Courtesy Chicago Historical Society

EUGENE VICTOR DEBS
1855-1926
Labor Organizer and Socialist

LINCOLN STEFFENS wrote to Brand Whitlock, mayor of Toledo, Ohio, during the 1908 Presidential campaign, "Vote for Debs. Don't try to decide the election; don't choose between the two evils. Vote for that sweet, good, passionate lover of mankind who offers hope and service, and leave the rest to God and the rest of us."

Eugene Victor Debs, for the third time Socialist party Presidential candidate of the United States, was running against the Democrat, William Jennings Bryan, also a three-time candidate, and William Howard Taft, the Republican nominee. In a sixty-five-day whistle-stop campaign, during which he spoke from the back of the train five to ten times daily, Debs toured the country bringing the message of socialism to the people. There were no loudspeakers; at times his voice cracked from the strain, and then his brother Theodore would substitute for him.

The idea of renting a campaign train—called the "Red Special" to epitomize the revolutionary spirit of the workers and the bloodshed and hardship they suffered—was conceived prior to the Socialist party convention in Chicago that year. The delegates at the convention enthusiastically voted approval, and Debs and William D. ("Big Bill") Haywood, an old-time Socialist, visited party locals to plead for the money necessary to conduct such a tour. Haywood would challenge, "Comrades, do you or don't you want to see our Debs and the Red Special?" And the "comrades" would drop nickels and dimes and quarters and dollars into the collection. By mid-August the Socialists had raised about sixteen thousand dollars and signed a contract with the railroad for the first half of the trip.

On the morning of August 31, 1908, the Red Special pulled out of Chicago's LaSalle Street station and headed west. Its first major stop was Davenport, Iowa, where, at a paid-admission evening meeting in the Opera House, Debs made his first major address of the journey.

"The working class has entered the political arena this year," he told his listeners, "with its own party and own platform which declares against the wage system and in favor of the social ownership of the modern machinery of production so that all shall have an opportunity to work the year round, so that industrial depression shall no longer doom millions to suffering and want in this land of fabulous abundance, so that the workers may not only have work, but leisure, that they may improve their minds, enlarge their vision and comprehension and live complete wholesome lives of really civilized human beings."

The newspapers, which generally had not given much publicity to previous Socialist campaigns, were captivated by the drama of the Red Special and gave the tour important coverage. The train, its baggage car filled with Socialist literature, arrived three hours late in Kansas City; but that evening a crowd of nearly three thousand people, each paying admission, greeted Debs at Convention Hall, where he lashed out at the capitalist system and its Presidential nominees Taft and Bryan. Taft had been selected by President Theodore Roosevelt as his successor because Taft was neither an extreme conservative nor an extreme progressive. Bryan, again the nominee of the Democratic party, had first captured the party's nomination in 1896 with his stirring "Cross of Gold" speech which proposed the free coinage of silver at a time when the country was divided between "gold" and "silver" advocates. In the 1908 campaign Bryan argued that he represented both labor and capital. To that statement Debs responded, "That's like riding two horses at the same time, each going in opposite directions."

"You produce all the wealth and have none of it," Debs told his working-class audience. "The capitalist class produces no wealth and has all of it. You make automobiles and—walk."

A voice from the audience shouted, "And get run over."

The train continued to run hours behind schedule because of the large crowds waiting to greet the candidate and talk with him at both scheduled and unscheduled stops.

At Glenwood Springs, Colorado, the mayor of the

town presided over the meeting. A ten-year-old girl came up to Debs, told him she was from Terre Haute, Debs's home town, and presented him with a bouquet of flowers. From then on, fruit and flowers were given to the candidate at most of the stops.

On the West Coast a middle-aged businessman, a fervent admirer of Debs, talked to one of the members of the Red Special committee about the violence committed against "leaders of the people." Wearing an automatic Colt on his belt, he said, "I often feel that someday they will do something to Gene. They are more afraid of him now than ever. But, by God, the man who hurts Gene, wherever he be, has got to answer to me personally."

From California, through Oregon, to Washington, the Red Special carried its tall, slim passenger to the crowds waiting to hear him—then it turned eastward. At one rural stop a group of schoolchildren visited the train. To his young listeners Debs described the lives of little children in big cities who had never even seen a live chicken; he spoke of the dedication of Socialists to make all children's lives brighter and happier. In Boston, old Faneuil Hall overflowed with people, and more than six thousand milled in the square outside. And back in Chicago, a crowd of sixteen thousand filled the Seventh Regiment Armory.

When the votes were counted after the election, Eugene Victor Debs, the 1908 Socialist party candidate for President of the United States, polled 420,973 votes, about 3 percent of the total vote cast. This was slightly more than the 402,321 he received in 1904, and more than four times the 96,116 he received in 1900, the first time he ran for President. But in the 1912 Presidential election, Debs received 897,011 votes, almost 6 percent of the total popular vote. This high vote was achieved despite the fact that the Republicans, under Taft, offered what was for them an unprecedented liberal program to balance the liberalism of Woodrow Wilson and his Democratic party and the Progressive party statements of Theodore Roosevelt, who had broken with the Republicans and was now leading the Bull Moose party.

The fifth and last time Debs was the Socialist party candidate was in 1920, while he was a prisoner in the Atlanta penitentiary for having opposed World War I. Out of approximately 26,700,000 votes cast for President, Socialist Eugene Victor Debs, a federal prisoner, received 919,799 votes. His campaign posters showed Debs in prison garb in front of a prison door.

A national figure long before he became a Presidential candidate, Eugene Victor Debs was the eldest son of the ten children of Jean Daniel and Marguerite Bettrich Debs. Jean Daniel, whose father had been a wealthy millowner in Alsace, France, loved French and German classics and prints. His only interest in his father's business was the small, gentle Marguerite Bettrich who worked in one of his father's mills. Over the objections of the elder Debs, the two became engaged. In 1848, after his father's death, Jean Daniel left his native land for America where Marguerite joined him a year later. Two days after her arrival they were married and moved to a little French colony in Terre Haute, Indiana.

The new husband tried his hand at various jobs, from working in the slaughterhouses to laying ties on the railroad. Finally he opened a grocery store and within a short time was earning a modest income.

Among Jean Daniel's favorite authors were Victor Hugo and Eugène Sue. When his first son was born on November 5, 1855, he was named Eugene Victor, after both writers. During Gene Debs's youth, the schooling he received on Sunday evenings at home when Jean Daniel tutored his children in the romantic literature of France and Germany—Hugo, Voltaire, Racine, Molière, Goethe—far outmatched what he learned in the Terre Haute school.

By the age of fifteen Gene had had enough of formal learning, and he left school to help contribute to the family income. He went to work in the Vandalia, Indiana, railroad paint shop, at first scraping paint from the sides of railroad cars, later painting stripes on the cars. One evening, while Debs was working, an engineer came into the paint shop complaining that he had no fireman for his train. The diligence with which the young Debs worked impressed the engineer, and the tall boy was given the job.

Marguerite Debs, however, concerned for her son's safety, was unhappy about his working on the trains.

It was generally known that in an effort to keep their costs down, the railroads were not too careful about safety measures. Some of the equipment used was unsafe, resulting in explosions and fires of the wooden cars, and worn rails in many instances were not replaced. In deference to his mother's concern for his safety, Debs left the railroad in October 1874 and became a clerk in a wholesale grocery firm, where he spent the next five years.

During this period Debs, always hungering for knowledge, purchased an encyclopedia on the installment plan, buying one volume each month and reading it, from the first page to the last, before the next arrived. His father gave him a copy of Voltaire's *Philosophical Dictionary*, which he read and reread. He subscribed to the New York *Tribune*, founded by Horace Greeley. American history fascinated him. Thomas Paine was his idol, and he read all he could about him. He was inspired by the revolutionary's words and challenged by Paine's century-old call to the American colonies, "These are the times that try men's souls."

While he was still working for the grocery firm, Debs became one of the founders and president of the Occidental Literary Club. Here he heard some of the great orators of the day, and here he gave his own early public speeches. As president, he persuaded the members to invite the brilliant orator and agnostic Robert G. Ingersoll to speak (see Ingersoll, pp. 175 ff.).

When Colonel Ingersoll arrived at the club, he was

greeted by a pouring rain and a group of worried young members who were afraid that no one would show up and that their treasury would not have the money to pay the popular lecturer. With his usual optimism and goodwill, the colonel told them he would let them off the contract if there were no audience and suggested they get something to eat before the lecture. As the welcoming committee of the Occidental Literary Club and their guest sat in the restaurant, the twenty-two-year-old Debs plied Ingersoll with questions about the art of public speaking, his agnosticism, his philosophy of liberty, and his politics.

The rain did not keep the people from coming. The hall was filled to capacity as Colonel Ingersoll delivered his lecture on "The Liberty of Man, Woman, and Child." It was the famed agnostic at his best, and the applause testified to its success.

Debs was attracted to Ingersoll's humanitarianism, his decisive way of thinking, and his brilliant performance on the lecture platform. The young man hoped that some day he too could hold the attention of an audience as Ingersoll did. He was captivated by Ingersoll's thoughts on religion and was sympathetic to them. After the meeting, he walked to the railroad station with Ingersoll, then unexpectedly decided to travel to Cincinnati with him. "The colonel was too magnetic, too kind and hospitable, and I simply had to go with him," Debs later explained to friends.

Ingersoll was only one of the many notables whom

the Occidental Literary Club brought to Terre Haute; among others were the poet James Whitcomb Riley, Wendell Phillips, the antislavery agitator, and Susan B. Anthony, the suffragette.

Terre Haute's reaction to Susan B. Anthony gave Debs his first exposure to group hostility. As he walked along the street with Miss Anthony, Debs became painfully aware that she "was an object of derision and contempt. It would not have required any great amount of egging on to have excited the people to drive her from the community." The evening was a failure. The citizens of Terre Haute were interested in neither Miss Anthony nor her views.

Debs continued to work in the wholesale grocery, but his allegiance was to railroading. When a meeting of the two-year-old Brotherhood of Locomotive Firemen was called in Terre Haute in 1875, Debs attended and volunteered to work with the union in his spare time. He became a charter member of the Terre Haute local and its first secretary, working nights and weekends for the union.

The railroad firemen responded slowly to organization despite long hours, poor wages, and dangers of the job, but Debs did not weaken in his purpose. He wrote for the union's periodical, *The Magazine*, with the Debs family home serving as his office. At the Brotherhood convention that year he was offered the job of secretary-treasurer and editor. Hesitantly, he accepted. His brother Theodore gave up his job in a haberdashery to become the union's bookkeeper, thus starting a lifetime association of social action for the two brothers who not only looked alike but thought alike. Theodore Debs adored Eugene, nine years his senior. His devotion and never-failing help strengthened their partnership in the causes for which they worked.

At the time Debs took over his new job, the Brotherhood treasury totaled not quite three hundred dollars and *The Magazine* was in debt for eighteen hundred. He assumed the responsibility of clearing the organization's debts. At the next convention, he was able to report that the Brotherhood had ninety-six lodges in its membership as against sixty at the last convention, the debt of the BLF had been paid off, its bank balance showed $1,175, and circulation of *The Magazine* had increased.

In 1879 the Democratic party nominated Eugene Victor Debs as city clerk, a choice the local newspaper hailed as "most admirable." The paper described Debs as "a finely-built young man of twenty five . . . active, hard-working, painstaking and inspired by a most laudable ambition to succeed in all he undertakes. He has a good voice to read the record of the Council and writes a neat, plain hand, with which to keep it. No one could be possessed of better qualifications." Gene Debs was elected and took office on January 1, 1880; he was reelected for a second two-year term. All during these years he continued to devote all his spare time to *The Magazine* and the Brotherhood.

Debs had little time for anything outside of his

job, his political activity, and the Brotherhood. Then, one evening in 1884, while visiting his sister, he met Katherine Metzel, the stepdaughter of a successful local druggist. He fell in love with her almost immediately, and within a year they were married. They spent their honeymoon in New York City, where they were entertained by Colonel Ingersoll.

Handsome and independent, Kate was a good choice for Debs. Although she came from a family of wealth, she did not interfere with his self-appointed goal of bettering the lot of the worker. She was drawn to his idealistic determination and the clarity with which he expressed his beliefs, many of which were alien to her. Her life with Debs was not easy. There were usually financial problems; both desired children and were saddened when they remained childless.

The same year Eugene and Kate married, the thirty-year-old bridegroom became a member of the Indiana state legislature. He sought this public position for one specific reason, namely, to introduce and pass a law to compensate railway employes injured on the job. While he succeeded in having the bill passed in the lower house, the Senate defeated it. Thoroughly disillusioned, Debs did not seek reelection. Instead, he turned all his attention to the Brotherhood and became its organizer and leader. In rain or snow, day or night, sleeping in the caboose or bunk, sharing the dinner pails of the firemen, Debs traveled the roads, speaking to railroad workers, agitating, urging them to join the union. Firemen, brakemen, conductors, track hands—everyone who worked on the railroad revered this idealist who gave voice to the suffering endured by countless workers and prodded them to unite to strengthen their union.

When Debs left on a trip his suitcase was full; when he returned it was usually empty as he had a habit of giving to those less fortunate not only the money in his pocket but even his clothes. He would return to Terre Haute exhausted and discouraged. Kate would soothe him and encourage him to relax, to spend time with his brother, his parents, his friends and neighbors.

This gentle man, who was to be charged by his enemies as aiming to destroy the home, insisted there were "two words in our language forever sacred to memory—Mother and Home." So much a sentimentalist was he about mother and home that Sunday evenings were always spent with his parents when he was in Terre Haute. He let nothing interfere with these occasions.

Debs considered the major problem facing railroad men to be a lack of cooperation between the various categories of railroad workers, for each trade had its own union which operated independently. He broke with the Brotherhood when he was convinced that it was not interested in working to protect all railroad workers. He believed a new type of union was necessary, and he worked toward that end. In June 1893 the American Railway Union, the one big industrial union of all railroad workers regardless of their craft, was founded at a meeting in Chicago. Debs was elected its first president with a salary of seventy-five dollars a month.

Almost immediately the new union won several minor contests with the railroads. Its first big battle, however, was in the spring of 1894 when the Great Northern railway cut wages for the third time in less than a year. The ARU warned the company that unless the wage cuts were immediately restored the line would be struck. The company refused, and a strike was called. Not a train on the Great Northern moved, and after eighteen days the workers triumphantly returned to their trains with "97½ percent" of what they had demanded granted.

A few months later the workers of the Pullman Palace Car Company turned to the American Railway Union for help. The Pullman company, headed by its founder, George Pullman, manufactured luxury sleeping cars for railroads. George Pullman had built homes, churches, and schools for his employees in what he considered an ideal community—Pullman, Illinois—located just south of Chicago. But the Panic of 1893 affected the sales and profits of the Pullman company. While rents and other costs of the Pullman employees living in the company town remained the same, wages were cut from 33 to 50 percent. The wage cut was the company's answer to the depression. The employees, unable to meet payments, fell deeper and deeper into debt to George Pullman.

Members of the ARU suggested their union call a

sympathy strike with the Pullman workers. Debs opposed this because he felt the ARU was neither strong enough nor disciplined enough to conduct an effective strike against Pullman despite its victory with the Great Northern railway. Debs was overruled; the convention voted a $2,000 relief fund and a boycott of Pullman cars, which meant that ARU members would not work on any train to which the Pullman sleeper was attached. Once the strike was called, Debs enthusiastically supported it. At the same time, he urged members to refrain from violence; again and again, in speeches, letters, and telegrams to all ARU locals, he repeatedly urged the strikers to be nonviolent. Despite Debs's pleas against violence, railroad traffic was forcibly interrupted, the movement of freight cars was obstructed in the railroad yards, and some of the cars were burned. The railroad asked for an injunction forbidding the union "from in any way or manner interfering with, hindering, obstructing, or stopping" business in twenty-one railroads listed in the injunction. This was granted by a federal court.

Debs's reaction to the restraining order was, "Injunctions can't move trains."

The executive board of the ARU voted to ignore the injunction because it considered that submission would not only end the strike but would mean the death of trade unionism in the United States. Then, to the dismay of Debs and over the protests of Illinois Governor John P. Altgeld, President Grover Cleveland ordered federal troops to Chicago.

Of the arrival of federal troops, Debs commented, "Troops cannot move trains."

Governor Altgeld later explained that he did not order state troops to Chicago because at no time had anybody "in Cook County, whether official or private citizen, asked to have their assistance, or even intimated in any way that their assistance was desired or necessary."

The arrival of federal troops increased the tension within the city, and violence became more common. Spectators charged that the federal troops provoked many of the incidents. However, the injunction—and the troops—did combine to defeat the strikers. Debs and the other strike leaders were indicted and charged with violation of the injunction and with conspiracy in restraining trade and obstructing the movement of the mails.

"Stand by your principles, regardless of consequences," Debs's parents wrote to their son.

Eugene Field, the famous children's poet and author of "Little Boy Blue," had written to Debs during the strike, "I hear you are to be arrested. When that time comes you will need a friend. I want to be that friend."

In the meantime, Clarence Darrow resigned as corporation counsel of Chicago and North Western Railway to become the attorney for Eugene Victor Debs and the ARU (see Darrow, pp. 96 ff.).

The first case, that of criminal conspiracy under the Sherman Anti-Trust Act, was called in January 1895 in the federal court in Chicago. With the trial practically completed, one of the twelve jurors fell ill. The defense wanted to continue with eleven men, but the government asked for a mistrial and the judge dismissed the jury. Finally, the case itself was dropped. Later it was learned that the jury had been eleven to one for acquittal.

The trial for violating the injunction followed. This time there was no jury. With the same evidence presented by the prosecution as in the conspiracy trial, Debs and the other men were sentenced to six months in jail at Woodstock, Illinois, by the judge who was one of the two federal judges originally granting the injunction.

From jail, Debs issued a statement: "In going to jail for participation in the late strike, I have no apologies to make nor regrets to express. . . . I would not change places with [the judge], and if it is expected that six months or even six years in jail will purge me of contempt, the punishment will fail of its purpose."

The prison term did not "purge" Debs. Instead, it introduced him to socialism.

"It was at this time," Debs later wrote, "when the first glimmerings of socialism were beginning to penetrate, that Victor L. Berger—and I have loved him ever since—came to Woodstock, as if a providential instrument, and delivered the first impassioned message of socialism I had ever heard—the very first to set the 'wires humming in my system.' "

Berger, a veteran Socialist, gave Debs a copy of *Das Kapital* by Karl Marx. It was not *Das Kapital*, however, which stimulated Debs's interest in socialism;

neither the book nor Marx moved him. In fact, he found the book dull reading. Debs became a Socialist and a pacifist because he was motivated by a love for his fellowmen and had a desire to help them overcome the evils of the economic system. It was Berger—the Milwaukee schoolteacher and Socialist editor and publisher—talking with Debs for hours in his Woodstock cell, who aroused his interest in socialism as a political movement.

On the morning of November 22, 1895, Debs was released from the Woodstock prison. His brother Theodore came to escort him home, where Kate was patiently waiting. When they arrived at the Woodstock town square, they were greeted by a delegation of trade unionists all wildly cheering Debs and waving American flags. They carried their labor leader on their shoulders, and then all boarded a special train for Chicago where thousands greeted them at the depot. Before going home to Terre Haute, Debs spoke to a packed auditorium at the Battery D Armory in Chicago. He confided to a cheering audience, "I am not certain whether this is an occasion for rejoicing or lamentation. I confess to a serious doubt as to whether this day marks my deliverance from bondage to freedom or my doom from freedom to bondage."

He again defended his actions in the Pullman strike: "I am not disposed to shrink from the fullest responsibility for my acts. I have had time for meditation and reflection and I have no hesitancy in declaring that under the same circumstances I would pursue precisely the same policy. So far as my acts are concerned, I have neither apology nor regrets."

Though the seeds of socialism were planted in Debs while he was in jail, he nevertheless campaigned for William Jennings Bryan, the Democratic candidate in the 1896 Presidential election. He also campaigned for John Peter Altgeld who was seeking reelection as governor of Illinois, and for Clarence Darrow, a candidate for the United States Congress. All three were defeated.

Debs's official affiliation with the Socialist movement came in June 1897 at the last convention of the American Railway Union. Not many members were present, and those who were there agreed to adjourn and then convene as the first convention of the Social Democracy. Within a year a split had occurred between the political activists and the philosophical reformers of the party, and the political activists withdrew to form the Social Democratic Party of America. Gene Debs gave his full support to the SDA, describing it as "not a reform party but a revolutionary party . . . unequivocally for the collective ownership and control of all the means of wealth production and distribution—in a word, Socialism."

The SDA eventually became the Socialist Party of America. As the movement split, defined, and redefined its program, Debs remained the spokesman for socialism in the United States. In the national elections of 1900, officials of the SDA insisted that Debs be the party's nominee for President; there were many factions and only he could unite them. Debs refused, as he had four years earlier when the Populist party wanted him to be its candidate. He had no desire to run for public office; he was a labor organizer, he argued, not a Presidential candidate. He pleaded that he had no political ambitions, that he could be far more effective in his present activities. But the party officials persisted, and he was finally persuaded to start the first of his five campaigns for President of the United States on the Socialist ticket.

Debs continued to speak out on the issues of the day as he supported strikes, challenged injustice, championed the cause of the workers—black and white. He was adamant in his belief in equality for labor, and this stubbornness kept him going, despite the sometimes violent opposition to his views. When he had been a Democratic member of the Indiana state legislature, he voted, unsuccessfully, with the Republicans for equal rights for the black man as well as for the extension of women's suffrage. Debs had no prejudices, and when to his dismay he encountered bias toward the Negro within the Socialist ranks, he wrote in the November 1903 issue of the *International Socialist Review:*

"The Negro, given economic freedom, will not ask the white man any social favors . . . there is no Negro question outside of the labor question—the working class struggle. Our position as Socialists and as a party is perfectly plain. We have simply to say: 'The class struggle is colorless.' . . .

"For myself, my heart goes to the Negro and I make no apology to any white man for it. In fact, when I see the poor, brutalized, outraged black victim, I feel a burning sense of guilt for his intellectual poverty and moral debasement that makes me blush for the unspeakable crimes committed by my own race."

In reply, Debs received a letter signed, "So far a staunch member of the Socialist party." The writer pointed out that Abraham Lincoln had asserted that "there is a physical difference between the white and black races, which I believe will forever forbid them living together on terms of social and political equality."

Debs responded in an article titled "The Negro and His Nemesis," in the January 1904 issue of the Socialist magazine: "Abraham Lincoln was a noble man, but he was not an abolitionist, and what he said in reference to the Negro was with due regard to his circumscribed environs, and, for the time, was doubtless the quintessence of wisdom, but he was not an oracle who spoke for all coming ages, and we are not bound by what he thought prudent to say in a totally different situation half a century ago. . . . The normal Negro has ambition to rise. This is to his credit and ought to be encouraged. He is not asking, nor does he need, the white man's social favors. He can regulate his personal associations with entire satisfaction to himself, without Anglo-Saxon concessions.

"Socialism will strike the economic fetters from his body and he himself will do the rest."

In 1905, Debs was one of the organizers, with William D. ("Big Bill") Haywood, of the Industrial Workers of the World. Haywood was also a Socialist and the militant secretary-treasurer of the Western Federation of Miners. Debs looked to the IWW as the realization of his dream of one big union of all workers. "They charge us with being assembled here for the purpose of disrupting the union movement," he told the delegates at the first convention of the IWW. "It is already disrupted . . . we are here today for the purpose of uniting the working class." He was bitter at the lack of effort by the American Federation of Labor to organize all workers into one union. Its failure to do so, he believed, permitted one craft union to scab on another, thus hurting the entire labor movement.

In time Debs dropped out of the IWW. He believed in political action, while Haywood and the others in the IWW put their tactical strength in such direct action as the strike, boycott, and, in some instances, sabotage. Debs approved the strike and boycott, but he opposed sabotage, which he believed led to violence. He argued for a working class political party as epitomized by the Socialist party. The IWW frowned on this.

Despite their differences, Debs respected the IWW and its idea of one big union. Many years after he left the organization—during World War I when Haywood and more than one hundred members were on trial in Chicago charged with hindering the United

States war effort—Debs declared: "Few men have the courage to say a decent word in favor of the IWW. I have. . . . I have great respect for the IWW. Far greater than I have for their infamous detractors."

By 1914 Debs's attention was almost exclusively directed to international affairs. He campaigned tirelessly against the war in Europe and any United States participation in it. "I am opposed to every war but one . . . and that is the worldwide war of the social revolution. In that war I am prepared to fight in any way the ruling class may make necessary, even to the barricades," said the pacifist who hated bloodshed but emotionally defended social revolution.

The 1916 election issues in the United States centered mainly around the war. The constant refrain of the Democratic party was that President Woodrow Wilson "kept us out of war," and this issue won votes from many independents, Socialists, and Progressives.

The reelected President Wilson made overtures to Germany in an attempt to bring peace to Europe, but the moves were hopeless. In February 1917 the United States broke diplomatic relations with Germany, and two months later Congress declared war against the Imperial government of Germany.

With the entry of the United States into the war, the country was caught in a passionate nationalism in which anything German was decried. Music written by long-dead German composers was *verboten.* Statues of German personalities in public places were smeared with paint; pacifists were imprisoned; periodicals which voiced objection to the war were banned; antiwar meetings were broken up by police and vigilantes. In a surge of patriotism, even hamburgers became "Liberty Steaks."

Gene Debs continued to insist that only capitalists would profit from this war, as this was a war neither for national defense nor for labor. The Socialist party members generally agreed and called an emergency convention of the party which endorsed an antiwar stand. Debs was elated with the party's resolution.

On his way to Canton, Ohio, where he was to speak at the Ohio State Socialist convention, Debs stopped off at the Stark County Workhouse to visit three of his comrades who were serving prison terms for their opposition to the draft law.

He referred to this visit in his opening remarks at the convention. He then observed, "I realize that in speaking to you this afternoon, there are certain limitations placed upon the right of free speech. I must be extremely careful, prudent, as to what I say, and even more careful and prudent as to how I say it." The crowd laughed. "I may not be able to say all I think; but I am not going to say anything that I do not think. I would rather a thousand times be a free soul in jail than to be a sycophant and coward in the streets." The crowd applauded and shouted agreement.

He talked of the German Junkers and Prussian militarism, of Socialist opposition to them as well as to the Junkers in the United States. Then he turned to socialism, its future. His tall lean body perched forward, his hands outstretched for emphasis, he said, "Socialism is a growing idea. It is spreading over the entire face of the earth. It is as vain to resist it as it would be to arrest the sunrise on the morrow. It is coming, coming, coming all along the line. Can you not *see* it? . . . It is the mightiest movement in the history of mankind."

Debs talked for almost two hours. As the meeting adjourned, Department of Justice agents stopped the younger Socialists and asked to see their draft registry cards.

Two weeks later, Eugene Victor Debs was arrested while he was speaking before a meeting of Socialists in Cleveland, an arrest resulting from an indictment by a federal grand jury which charged Debs with violation of the Espionage Act. The Canton speech was the basis of the charge. He also was charged with attempting to "obstruct the recruiting and enlistment service of the United States" by that speech.

Clarence Darrow offered to help in Debs's defense, but the militant Socialist refused the offer because of Darrow's prowar feelings. When the government completed its case, the court was informed that the defense had no witnesses and Debs would plead his own case to the jury of "responsible and wealthy" citizens of merchants and farmers.

"Men talk about holy wars. There are none," Debs told the court. "It is the ruling classes that make war upon one another, and not the people. In all the history of this world the people have never yet declared a war."

He admitted the truth of all the prosecution's testimony as well as the accuracy of the speech as reported in the courtroom. "I have been accused of having obstructed the war. I admit it. Gentlemen, I abhor war. I would oppose the war if I stood alone. . . . What you may choose to do to me will be of small consequence after all. I am not on trial here. There is an infinitely greater issue that is being tried today in this court, though you may not be conscious of it. American institutions are on trial here before a court of American citizens. The future will tell."

On the following day the judge instructed the jury, and for six hours they deliberated. Their verdict: "Guilty as charged in the indictment."

The judge asked Debs whether he had anything to say before sentence was passed. Gene Debs rose from his chair. He began to talk as he walked toward the bench.

"Your Honor, years ago I recognized my kinship with all living beings, and I made up my mind that I was not one bit better than the meanest of earth. I said then, I say now, that while there is a lower class, I am in it; while there is a criminal element, I am of it; while there is a soul in prison, I am not free."

He again declared his allegiance to socialism and his opposition to the present form of government. "Your Honor, I ask no mercy. I plead for no immunity. I realize that finally the right must prevail. I never more clearly comprehended than now the great struggle between the powers of greed on the one hand and upon the other the rising hosts of freedom. . . . Let the people take heart and hope everywhere, for the cross is bending, the midnight is passing, and joy cometh with the morning."

The judge and Debs looked at each other for a moment in silence. Then the judge said, "I am a conserver of the peace and a defender of the Constitution of the United States." He denounced as enemies those who "within our borders" would "strike the sword from the hand of the nation while she is engaged in defending herself against a foreign and brutal power."

He sentenced Debs to serve ten years in the West Virginia State Penitentiary at Moundsville. Debs's bail continued at ten thousand dollars. The case was appealed to the United States Supreme Court, which upheld the conviction, and in mid-April 1919, five months after the Armistice, Debs traveled from Terre Haute to Cleveland, unescorted by guards, and surrendered to federal authorities to begin the journey to Moundsville. Two months later he was transferred to the Atlanta federal prison where he remained for two and one-half years, until his sentence was commuted.

In 1920 a delegation of the Socialist party visited Debs in prison. "Comrade Debs," they said, "once again the Socialist party wants you to be its candidate for President of the United States."

"I will be our party's candidate," Convict Number

9653 told the delegation. "I will be a candidate at home. It won't be as strenuous or tiresome a campaign, and my managers and opponents can always locate me." His home address: Federal Penitentiary, Atlanta, Georgia.

During this time, a campaign had been initiated to win the release of various political prisoners, including Debs, who were serving jail sentences because of their opposition to World War I. The attorney general of the United States recommended a commutation of Debs's sentence, but President Wilson refused to act. A similar appeal was later made to President Warren G. Harding, Wilson's successor. Harding's attorney general recommended a commutation, and the Republican President, unlike his Democratic predecessor, commuted the sentences of Debs and twenty-three other political prisoners.

The New York Times carried a page-one story on December 26, 1921. Its headline read:

DEBS IS RELEASED,
PRISONERS JOINING
CROWD IN OVATION

Debs left the prison amidst cheers and goodbyes from the other prisoners, many of whom felt their lives had been profoundly changed by the gentle, warm revolutionary who spoke to them of love and justice.

Gene Debs had to make one stop before he went home to Kate and Terre Haute: President Harding had asked to see him. Although the two men visited for twenty minutes, there has never been an official report on the meeting. Debs said he found the President to be "a kind gentleman, one who I believe possesses humane impulses. We understand each other."

Darrow, commenting on President Harding's pardon of Debs, said, "I had always admired Woodrow Wilson and distrusted Harding . . . still, Mr. Wilson, a scholar and an idealist . . . kept Debs in prison; and Mr. Harding . . . unlocked the door." Many agreed with Darrow when he observed: "So far as I am concerned, I never think of . . . Harding . . . without saying to myself: 'Well, [he] pardoned Debs!' "

The day after Debs's visit with President Harding, he left for Terre Haute where he was greeted by a torchlight parade and carried high in the air to a waiting wagon, then home to Kate, their first meeting in three years.

Eugene Victor Debs was sixty-six years old. His health was broken. He suffered from rheumatism, lumbago, stomach trouble which was intensified by the poor prison food, recurrent headaches, and heart trouble. A lecture tour was interrupted because of exhaustion. Kate nursed him and he recovered, only to suffer another attack. He continued his work—lecturing and writing, editing the new Socialist weekly, the *American Appeal*—but he was failing.

On October 15, 1926, the Socialist agitator fell into a coma, and five days later, on October 20, he died. At his bedside were Kate and his brother Theodore.

Eugene Debs's career saw the rise of the industrial

union movement. He saw his Socialist party poll almost a million votes in a Presidential election, and then decline because of internecine struggles which resulted in a split within the party and the formation of the Communist party soon after the Russian Revolution. With little interest in doctrinal matters, Debs remained aloof from the party strife. He believed in political action by the working class and the Socialist party as the representative of that class. He believed in the class struggle, but he always distrusted violence and insisted that the end must be accomplished by peaceful and parliamentary means.

After his death the Communist party claimed him as one of their own, but he was never a Communist either in affiliation or in his sympathies. He could feel empathy with the aims of the Russian Revolution —bread, peace, and freedom—but he would not condone violence to attain those aims or to maintain them.

The body of Eugene Victor Debs lay in state at the Labor Temple in Terre Haute for two days before it was shipped to Indianapolis. Labor delegations from all over the country came to pay their last respects to the man who had told them, "I am not a labor leader. I don't want you to follow me or anyone else. If you are looking for a Moses to lead you out of the capitalist wilderness, you will stay right where you are. I would not lead you into this promised land if I could, because if I could lead you in, someone else would lead you out."

In the spring of 1964, a group of labor men and Socialists, including Norman Thomas, dedicated the Debs home in Terre Haute as a memorial to him. The General Assembly of Indiana designated the home as a Eugene Victor Debs Memorial and resolved to "keep alive the principles of liberty, freedom, and equality for which Eugene Victor Debs so ably and freely dedicated his life."

Clarence Seward Darrow

CLARENCE SEWARD DARROW
1857-1938
Lawyer and Humanist

ON MARCH 13, 1958, the twentieth aniversary of the death of Clarence Darrow, friends gathered at the memorial bridge named in his honor in Chicago's Jackson Park. At the exact moment that Darrow's friends tossed a wreath into the lagoon in memory of the famed attorney, his most famous client, Nathan Leopold, walked out of the Illinois Stateville Penitentiary paroled from a sentence of life plus ninety-nine years.

Darrow had told the judge in this murder-kidnapping case, as he pleaded for mercy for Leopold and his friend, Richard Loeb: "I do not know how much salvage there is in these two boys. . . . I will be honest with this court as I have tried to be from the beginning. I know that these boys are not fit to be at large. I believe they will not be until they pass through the next stage of life, at forty-five or fifty." Leopold was fifty-two years old when he was paroled.

The Leopold and Loeb case made international headlines in 1924. The two boys were brilliant honor students: Leopold at eighteen had just graduated from the University of Chicago; the seventeen-year-old Loeb was a graduate of the University of Michigan.

Their fathers were prominent Chicago businessmen, both millionaires.

Dickie Loeb was fascinated with crime and detective stories; he yearned to be a master criminal and to commit the perfect crime of kidnapping, murder, and ransom. He wanted Leopold, his friend and confidant, to help. They had no specific victim in mind. They considered first Loeb's younger brother, next the grandson of a Chicago industrialist, then a friend. But on Ellis Avenue, in their neighborhood, they saw Robert Franks, a distant relative of Loeb's, and invited the fourteen-year-old youngster into the car they had rented. As they drove through the familiar streets, Loeb struck the Franks boy on the head with a chisel four times. Before they stuffed the body into a culvert next to the railroad tracks on the far south side of Chicago, they poured hydrochloric acid over it in an attempt to avoid identification. The kidnapping and the murder were accomplished; now to collect the ransom money and complete the perfect crime.

Leopold called the Franks home and, reaching the mother, told her that her son had been kidnapped and was safe. The special delivery letter which arrived at the Franks home the next morning explained, "This is strictly a commercial proposition," and demanded ten thousand dollars in ransom money. Before Mr. Franks left to make the payment, however, the body of his son was discovered and identified. Authorities found Leopold's horn-rimmed glasses near the body, and soon after their arrest the boys confessed.

The Loeb and Leopold families came to Darrow in the early morning hours and begged the attorney to save the boys' lives. Now, at age sixty-seven, Darrow, who had spent his life defending the poor, the weak, the dispossessed, undertook the defense of two rich boys who needed him because of a brutal and senseless murder. All his life Darrow opposed killing—whether by individuals or by the state in retribution for a crime. In the Loeb-Leopold case, he had a national platform from which to speak out against capital punishment, to explain his theories on the cause and treatment of crime.

Newspaper headlines read, "Millions to defend killers."

The state's attorney proclaimed, "I have a hanging case."

On July 21, 1924, the case of the State of Illinois versus Nathan Leopold, Jr., and Richard Loeb opened in the courtroom of John R. Caverly, chief justice of the Criminal Court of Cook County. A startled courtroom heard Darrow ask the judge for permission to change the boys' plea from not guilty to guilty.

With the change of plea, Darrow asked the court's permission to present "evidence in mitigation of punishment." He called four alienists, now called psychiatrists, to substantiate his contention that the boys were "mentally diseased." For the first time, psychiatric evidence was placed in a court record in a murder trial as part of the defense. The state countered with its own alienists who disagreed.

The judge, who was hearing the case without a jury, listened as the district attorney thundered, "Darrow says that hanging does not stop murder. I think he is mistaken. The law says in extreme circumstances death shall be the penalty. If I were in the legislature I might vote against such a law. I don't know. But as a judge I have no right to put aside that law. I have no right to be a judicial anarchist, even if Clarence Darrow is an anarchistic advocate."

The charge of anarchism against Darrow was an old one. He admitted he was a philosophical anarchist "impressed" with the teachings of Peter Kropotkin and Leo Tolstoy, who advocated political freedom, mutual aid, and cooperation without government. Further, Darrow had told prisoners in the Cook County jail that he did not "in the least believe in crime" as the word is understood and that people were not in jail because they deserved to be but because they could not avoid it.

"Isn't this a dangerous philosophy, akin to anarchism?" asked the newspapers.

This same "dangerous philosophy," charged the state's attorney, permeated Darrow's defense of Leopold and Loeb.

The day Darrow began his summation to the judge, thousands jammed the corridors in an attempt to get into the courtroom to hear him. The frenzied mob made it difficult for even Darrow, the prosecutor, and the families of the defendants to enter.

"Your Honor," Darrow began his summation, "it

has been almost three months since the great responsibility of this case was assumed by my associates and myself." His hair falling across his forehead, thumbs hooked onto his suspenders, Darrow looked exhausted, tired of human suffering. "Your Honor, I am willing to confess that it has been three months of great anxiety," he said. He pointed out that the anxiety was not due primarily to the facts of this case but to the almost unheard-of publicity it had received.

He then disposed of the charge of a million-dollar defense: "We announced to the public that no excessive use of money would be made in this case, neither for lawyers nor for psychiatrists, nor in any other way. We have faithfully kept that promise. . . . The attorneys, at their own request, have agreed to take such amount as the officers of the Chicago Bar Association may think is proper in this case.

"If we fail in this defense," he asserted, "it will not be for lack of money. It will be on account of money. . . .

"I am not pleading so much for these boys as I am for the infinite number of others to follow, those who perhaps cannot be as well defended as these have been, those who may go down in the tempest without aid. It is of them I am thinking, and for them I am begging this court not to turn backward toward the barbarous and cruel past. . . .

"Your Honor stands between the past and the future. . . . I am pleading for the future; I am pleading for a time when hatred and cruelty will not control the hearts of men, when we can learn by reason and judgment and understanding and faith that all life is worth saving, and that mercy is the highest attribute of man."

Darrow's voice faded into silence; his eyes were filled with tears. The silence of the courtroom was penetrated by sobs from the audience. The judge, too, had tears in his eyes.

Judge Caverly deliberated two weeks before he sentenced each boy to life imprisonment for the murder charge and ninety-nine years for the kidnapping.

Twelve years later a fellow inmate killed Loeb in a prison brawl. Leopold, paroled in March 1958, was released from parole five years later. Today he is married and lives in Castaner, Puerto Rico, where he is associate administrator of the Castaner General Hospital.

Clarence Seward Darrow was born in Kinsman, Ohio, the son of Amirus Darrow, town "infidel," who made his living as a furniture maker and town undertaker. Emily Darrow, Clarence's mother, was an ardent advocate of women's rights. Darrow's ancestry, on both sides, dated back to pre–Revolutionary War days in this country, and Darrow often frivolously commented that his ancestors went back to Adam and Eve.

Amirus Darrow had graduated from the Unitarian theological seminary in Meadville, Pennsylvania, but by the time he was ready to preach he found he had lost his faith. Nevertheless, he encouraged his children to attend Sunday school, where the young Clarence memorized parts of the Bible and sang hymns. Though poor, the family always had money for books, which were piled high on chairs and tables, on the floor and in bookcases. Thomas Jefferson, Voltaire, and Thomas Paine were widely read in the household.

The boy who grew up to be the nation's foremost defense attorney was the fifth of eight children. His formal education at the district school, then at the nearby academy, followed by a year at Allegheny College at Meadville and a year of law study at the University of Michigan, Ann Arbor, prepared him to read law in a lawyer's office in Youngstown, Ohio.

At the age of twenty-one, Darrow passed his bar examination and married Jessie Ohl, whom he had courted for more than four years. Although the Ohls were a prosperous family, Jessie was content to live modestly and quietly with her husband, and she seemed well suited to share the life of a small-town lawyer. In the small apartment which the couple rented, one room became Clarence's law office. His first cases in Kinsman and later in Andover and Ashtabula, Ohio, were simple ones—horse trades, disputes over boundary lines, private quarrels, fraudulent representations, now and then a criminal complaint which generally grew out of "the sale of liquor or watering milk." Slowly he built up a law practice. At the end of several years things were going very well for the young Darrows in Ashtabula, a much larger city than either Kinsman or Andover where they had previously lived. Darrow became active in politics and was elected city solicitor. By the age of thirty he was a small-town success.

In Ashtabula he also became acquainted with two books which helped to formulate his future philosophy. A banker introduced him to Henry George's *Progress and Poverty*, which argued that land and its wealth belonged to all and that a single tax on land-earnings—without recourse to any other taxes—would lead to economic and social justice. A police judge gave him John Peter Altgeld's masterly book on crime and criminals, *Our Penal Machinery and Its Victims*, in which Altgeld suggested that the way to cure crime was not by prisons but by learning the causes and then removing them.

The Darrows, having saved five hundred dollars, now decided to buy a house. When Darrow came to leave the deposit and accept the deed from the homeowners, the husband told Darrow that he could not sell the house to him. His wife refused to sign the deed because she did not think Darrow would be able to keep up the payments. A furious and humiliated Darrow responded that he did not want the house anyway, he had decided to move to Chicago.

The incident strengthened Darrow's belief in fate. He had said "Chicago" because he had a brother already living there and it was the first city to come to his mind. "There is no free will," he later insisted. "Had she signed that deed, I would probably be in Ashtabula now trying to meet overdue payments."

Soon after the family arrived in Chicago, Darrow joined the Single Tax Club, which provided a forum for young lawyers. In his early debates, Darrow attempted to imitate the oratorical rhythm, tempo, and poetical lilt of Robert Ingersoll. Then he decided that "I could not be Ingersoll and had no right to try and did not want to try . . . the best I could do was to be myself."

Darrow gave his first major speech at a Free Trade convention in Chicago at which Henry George was the featured attraction and the first speaker. When George concluded, there was a long applause, then people began to leave, for many had come only to hear him. Darrow turned to the chairman of the meeting and asked him to act quickly, before the hall was emptied altogether. The chairman introduced him, and, as the young orator started to speak, many of the people walking out returned to their seats. When Darrow finished he received an ovation, and Henry George, rushing up to him, enthusiastically congratulated him.

"I have talked from platforms countless times since then," Darrow wrote forty years later, "but never again have I felt that exquisite thrill of triumph after a speech."

DeWitt C. Cregier, the Democratic candidate for mayor of Chicago, heard Darrow at the Free Trade meeting. He was impressed with the lawyer and asked him to join his campaign, an invitation Darrow gladly accepted. After Cregier's election, he named Darrow his special assessment attorney. When the assistant corporation counsel resigned a few months later, Darrow was appointed to succeed him. From there, it was a short step up to city corporation counsel.

Four years later, Darrow resigned from the City of Chicago law department to become corporation counsel for the Chicago and Northwestern Railway Company. In 1894 the American Railway Union went out on strike against the Pullman Palace Car Company, a strike that affected the Chicago and Northwestern as well as other railway lines (see Debs, pp. 69 ff.).

Darrow saw no chance of settling the dispute amicably. He sided with the union men, and he wanted them to win. When he told the president of the Chicago and Northwestern that he was in sympathy with the strikers and therefore thought it best that he resign, the president, who admired Darrow greatly, insisted that he remain. Darrow agreed to stay, but only with the understanding that if either of them felt any embarrassment in the future they would take up the question again.

Soon train schedules were interrupted and mail cars delayed. The federal government named a special attorney to appear before the court to ask for an injunction against the union. The same lawyer also represented the Chicago, Milwaukee, and St. Paul Railway as well as the General Managers' Association, a management group made up of railroad companies.

Darrow charged the government with being unfair. It did not make sense to appoint a railroad man to represent the government, he asserted, just as it would not be right to give that job to an ARU lawyer.

When Eugene Victor Debs and other ARU officials were arrested for disregarding a federal injunction, Darrow was asked to join the union's legal defense. He agreed and resigned as corporation counsel for the railroad to represent Debs and the union. "Like the man who buys ten cents' worth of relief from the beggar on the street, I am buying relief too," he said in explanation of his action.

In the first trial, in which Debs and the other union men were charged with conspiracy, Darrow developed a technique which he was to use many times in the future. He not only defended his clients but turned the spotlight of publicity on the prosecution, and instead of presenting a defense he made an accusation.

"This is a historic case," he told the jury in the first Debs trial, "which will count much for liberty or against liberty. Conspiracy, from the days of tyranny in England down to the day the General Managers' Association used it as a club, has been the favorite weapon of every tyrant. . . . If the government does not, we shall try to get the general managers here to tell you what they know about conspiracy."

Darrow called Debs to the stand. Then he subpoenaed George Pullman because he wanted to contrast him with Debs; he felt the results would be favorable to his client. But the railroad magnate could not be found. Darrow used biting satire and direct jabs at Pullman's flight. Finally, a juror fell ill and the trial was adjourned, never to be called up again. The government now cited the union men for contempt in refusing to obey the injunction. The judge sentenced Debs and his fellow workers to six months in jail.

Two years later Darrow again defended union men,

this time in Oshkosh, Wisconsin, where the woodworkers walked off their jobs. They demanded a wage increase, a weekly instead of monthly pay period, abolition of child and female labor, and recognition of their union, the Amalgamated Woodworkers' International Union. For fourteen months the workers walked the picket line. Then one day Thomas I. Kidd, general secretary of the union, and two other members were arrested and charged with conspiring "to injure the business of the Paine Lumber Company, by means of a strike."

Darrow used the same technique in the Oshkosh case that he had developed in the Debs case, hurling accusations at the prosecution and insisting this was not a criminal case but "an episode in the great battle for human liberty." He read to the jury a list of rules which employees of the company were required to heed:

"Loud talking or shouting in or around the mill and factory cannot be allowed except in case of accident or fire.

"All employees are to be in their places when the bell rings and whistle blows for starting, and must not absent themselves except in cases of necessity.

"Employees who quit their places or the employ of this company without our consent or a reasonable notice of such intention, are subject to damages therefor; and such persons will not be paid until the next regular pay day following."

Yes, this was a conspiracy case, Darrow told the

jury, but the wrong people had been indicted. The defendants should not be the union men; the defendant should be George Paine, head of the Paine Lumber Company, who conspired with the state's attorney to arrest the union men.

"Ordinarily," the defense counsel told the jury, "men are brought into a criminal court for the reason that they are bad. Thomas I. Kidd is a defendant in these criminal proceedings because he loves his fellowmen."

In almost a whisper, Darrow concluded his summation on a theme heard many times in his pleas before a jury. "It has fallen to your lot, gentlemen, to be leading actors in one of the great dramas of human life. For some mysterious reason Providence has placed in your charge for today, aye for ages, the helpless toilers, the hopeless men, the dependent women and suffering children of the world."

The trial lasted three weeks. The twelve-man jury weighed the evidence for fifty minutes and returned a verdict of not guilty. Darrow's fee in the case was a token $250 and the promise by the union to publish his summation and distribute it to its members.

While Darrow continued to defend men and women charged with crime, his boundless energy turned also to lecturing and writing. His topics ranged from nonresistance and the social philosophy of Leo Tolstoy to the pessimism of Omar Khayyam; science, philosophy, literature, agnosticism, capital punishment—all engaged his interests.

He often dreamed of leaving his law practice to devote himself to writing. In 1925 he told a *New York Times* reporter, "I have reached the time when I have to turn away from the law and give my literary ambition a chance for expression." He contributed to many of the small insurgent magazines of his day, and was often embroiled in controversy as he raised his voice against injustice and brutality and the inequities of the law.

While working for William Randolph Hearst, publisher of the Chicago *Evening American*, he contributed a series of essays to the paper based on actual cases. Titled "Easy Lessons in Law," they illustrated how modern life warped the principles of justice. Darrow explained, "No remedy can be found for the unjust, unequal, oppressive laws under which we live except through public agitation and action."

His first book was a collection of critical essays, *A Persian Pearl and Other Essays*, published in 1899, which discussed such poets as Omar Khayyam, Robert Burns, and Walt Whitman, with all of whom he felt an emotional tie. *Resist Not Evil* (1903) was inspired by the nonresistance philosophies of Tolstoy whom he so much admired. *Farmington* appeared in 1904, the fictionalized story of Darrow's boyhood. *An Eye for an Eye* (1905) is probably one of the first novels of the proletarian school of literature. In this novel Darrow presented his case against capital punishment and again showed his compassion and understanding for the downtrodden. His writing style was simple, casual, with an unpolished sophistication which not only attracted readers but increased his lecture audience.

Though Darrow enjoyed the excitement of living in Chicago, his wife had never felt comfortable there. The lawyer delighted in the challenges offered by the city, its literary clubs, its political activities. He enjoyed debates, arguing, and discussing social theories. Jessie Darrow preferred a quiet home life. By 1897 they had drifted apart and were divorced "without contest or disagreement and without bitterness on either side." Their son, Paul, remained devoted to both of them.

In July 1903, six years after his divorce, Darrow married Ruby Hamerstrom, whom he had met after one of his lectures on Omar Khayyam. She was a feature writer for the Chicago *Evening Post*, sixteen years younger than he, attractive, vivacious, and intellectually his equal. She gave up her newspaper job to devote herself completely to his life and interests.

In the meantime, Darrow continued his legal career, always as a defense attorney defending both the strong and the weak, but never the strong against the weak.

In 1903 Darrow represented the United Mine Workers in arbitration hearings of the anthracite coal miners in Pennsylvania before a commission appointed by President Theodore Roosevelt.

At one point during these hearings, Darrow, relating the disadvantages of the union, told the commission that the mine owners "hire expert accountants;

they have got the advantage of us in almost every particular."

"Except the lawyers," interrupted the commission chairman.

As a result of the arbitration, the miners gained a 10 percent pay raise and an eight-hour workday as well as several million dollars in back pay.

In 1907 William D. ("Big Bill") Haywood, Charles H. Moyer, and George Pettibone, three officials of the Western Federation of Miners, were charged with the murder of the former governor of Idaho. The governor, a former union member, had been elected with labor support. Yet, during a miners' strike, he declared martial law and accused the Federation of Miners of using violence.

The miners were bitter against the former governor, now a sheep rancher and banker, and when he was murdered there were many who immediately felt that the Western Federation of Miners was responsible. Haywood, secretary-treasurer of the federation, Moyer, president, and Pettibone, once a union activist, were arrested and brought to trial. Harry Orchard, a man of questionable background, appeared as the chief witness against them. He not only confessed to the murder but accused the three union officials of having hired him to do the killing.

Labor leaders charged, "Frame-up!"

President Roosevelt called the three officials "undesirable citizens." In response to Roosevelt, Eugene Victor Debs and tens of thousands of union men throughout the country began to wear badges which read, "I am an Undesirable Citizen."

Haywood was the first to be tried. During the trial, Darrow called Orchard a "monstrous liar," a "perjured monster." The chief prosecutor, William Borah, who later became a liberal senator from Idaho, commented to the court that if the "monstrous liar" had not turned state's evidence "the eminent counsel from Chicago would be defending him with all the eloquence he possessed instead of denouncing him as the most despicable monster on earth."

In his summation to the jury, Darrow stressed that Haywood, Moyer, and Pettibone were not his "greatest concern," that other men before them had died for the cause of labor. "Men have been martyrs to a holy cause since the world began. Wherever men have looked upward and onward, forgotten their selfishness, struggled for humanity, worked for the poor and the weak, they have been sacrificed. It is not for Haywood alone that I speak. I speak for the poor, for the weak, for the weary."

The case went to the jury the same evening Darrow concluded his plea. The next morning the jury returned the verdict of not guilty. Pettibone was tried next, and the verdict in his case, too, was not guilty. The case against Moyer was dismissed.

In 1911 Darrow took on the case of the McNamara brothers who were charged with having dynamited the Los Angeles *Times* building (see Steffens, pp. 40 ff.). The disappointments that beset this undertaking were climaxed when the state alleged that Darrow, through one of his investigators in the case, had tried to bribe and influence two jurors. Darrow faced not only a one- to ten-year prison term on the charge of bribery but a sentence of not more than five years or a fine of five thousand dollars on the charge of having attempted to influence prospective jurors. Darrow himself now needed an attorney for the defense.

When the case of Clarence Darrow versus the State of California opened on May 15, 1912, at the defense table next to Darrow were Earl Rogers and Jerry Geisler. Rogers was at that time the nation's foremost criminal attorney, and Geisler, who later became one of Hollywood's famous attorneys for the movie colony, was a law clerk in Rogers's office.

Rogers and Darrow agreed that Darrow would make the final plea, and on August 14, 1912, Darrow began his summation in his own defense, to a jury made up of orange growers, ranchers, and businessmen, in a courtroom crowded with spectators.

"I have committed one crime," Darrow told the jury. "I have stood for the weak and the poor. I have stood for the men who toil." He spotlighted the social and political forces which were working to destroy him. The McNamara case was a hard fight, Darrow continued. "I would have walked from Chicago across the Rocky Mountains and over the long dreary desert to lay my hand upon the shoulder of J. B. McNamara and tell him not to place dynamite in the *Times* building.

"But I am not going to judge him. He believed in a cause, and he risked his life in that cause. Whether rightly or wrongly, it makes no difference with the motives of the man. I would not have done it. You would not have done it. But judged in the light of his motives, which is the only way that man can be judged—and for that reason only the infinite God can judge a human being—judged in the light of his motives, I cannot condemn the man, and I will not."

Darrow's plea to the jury, which has been called "one of the most masterly ever heard in an American courtroom," explained his own philosophy as well as the social act of the McNamara brothers. Always he tried to understand what led one man to act in a certain way and another to act in a different way. He would judge neither.

After thirty-four minutes, the jury's verdict: not guilty. With practically the same evidence as in the first case, a second jury could reach no agreement on the second charge of attempting to influence prospective jurors. It was dismissed, and finally the charge itself was dropped.

Darrow's two-year absence on the McNamara case and the defense of his reputation had cost him more than personal anguish. When he returned to Chicago he found his law practice gone. Neither the corporations nor the labor unions he represented before leaving for Los Angeles came to his office, nor did new clients seek his services. At the age of fifty-six, Darrow, tired and disillusioned, practically penniless, decided he was through with the law. The lecture platform offered immediate income, since people still enjoyed hearing him speak. Darrow engaged an agent and traveled the lecture circuit.

When Peter Sissman, a Russian immigrant whom Darrow had taken into his office twenty years earlier, heard that Darrow was going to give up law, he asked the attorney to share his practice. Darrow was hesitant. With Sissman's insistence, however, he finally agreed to a partnership.

During the first year, the new partner spent much of his time on the lecture platform. Very slowly clients began to come, and in due time Darrow reestablished an active law practice. As before, he never turned away anybody who needed his help, except for the habitual criminal whom he refused to defend more than once. In more than half of his cases he charged no fee.

When World War I broke out, Darrow, the pacifist, became convinced that the Germans were the aggressors when they marched through Belgium. Though he supported the war effort, Darrow spent days and nights rushing to jails and to the courts helping many who were arrested for their protest against the war.

During the "Red hysteria" in 1920, Darrow defended twenty Communist Labor party members accused of advocating the overthrow of the government by force. He explained that when he had become a lawyer, he had determined that there never should be a case, no matter how unpopular or whatever the feeling against it, that he would refuse to defend, and he had never done so. "When the cry is the loudest the defendant needs the lawyer most. . . . I shall not argue to you whether the defendants' ideas are right or wrong," he told the jury. "I am not bound to believe them right in order to take their case, and you are not bound to believe them right in order to find them not guilty. . . . I am here to defend their right to express their opinions."

He then warned, "You can only protect your liberties in this world by protecting the other man's freedom. You can only be free if I am free."

The jury thought otherwise and found the twenty defendants guilty. The Illinois Supreme Court affirmed the lower court, with Chief Justice Orrin Carter dissenting. Governor Len Small used Justice Carter's dissent to pardon the defendants before they had served a day of their sentence.

In 1922 Darrow published a book, *Crime: Its Causes and Treatment*, which became the basis of his later defense of Leopold and Loeb.

A year after the sensational trial of the two boys, Darrow again was involved in a world-famous case where he challenged the anti-evolution law in Tennessee. The law denied the right to teach Charles Darwin's theory of evolution in a public school classroom.

When William Jennings Bryan, for whom Darrow had campaigned in three Presidential elections, joined the prosecution of Thomas Scopes, a twenty-four-year-old high school teacher in Dayton, Tennessee, who had discussed evolution in a biology class, Darrow offered his services to the defense.

Bryan was probably more responsible for the anti-evolution law than anyone else; he had long urged Southern legislatures to pass such a law. As a Fundamentalist, Bryan believed in a literal interpretation of the Bible. He and other Fundamentalists felt that evolution challenged the old religious beliefs and would lead to atheism and agnosticism. Bryan contended that an "insolent minority" was forcing "irreligion upon the children under the guise of teaching science," and he expressed his alarm by a frantic defense of evangelical Protestantism.

Darrow, on the other hand, saw the anti-evolution law as hampering education and putting it in danger from "religious fanatics," and he questioned its constitutionality. He argued that "if today you can take a thing like evolution and make it a crime to teach it in the public school, tomorrow you can make it a crime to teach it in the private school, and in the next year you can make it a crime to teach it from the hustings or in the church. At the next session you may ban books and the newspapers. Soon you may set Catholic against Protestant and Protestant against Protestant, and try to foist your own religion upon the minds of men. . . . After a while, Your Honor, it is the setting of man against man and creed against creed until, with flying banners and beating drums, we are marching backward to the glorious ages of the sixteenth century when bigots lighted fagots to burn the men who dared to bring any intelligence and enlightenment and culture to the human mind."

Darrow intended to call several scientists to the stand as expert witnesses to define evolution and show that any intelligent interpretation of the Bible was not in conflict with any story of creation. Ready to testify for the defense were such scientists as Maynard Metcalf of Johns Hopkins University; Kirtley F. Mather of Harvard; Winterton C. Curtis, zoologist, University of Missouri; Dr. Fay-Cooper Cole, anthropologist, University of Chicago.

The court ruled against such testimony. Many of the newspapermen left Dayton believing that the judge's ruling ended the case. But the defense had a surprise request—that Mr. Bryan be called as an expert witness on the Bible. Bryan agreed to testify.

"Do you claim that everything in the Bible should be literally interpreted?" Darrow asked the witness.

"I believe everything in the Bible should be accepted as it is given there," Bryan answered firmly.

"But when you read that Jonah swallowed the whale—or that the whale swallowed Jonah—excuse me, please—how do you literally interpret that?"

"My impression," stated Bryan, "is that it says fish; but it does not make so much difference; I believe in a God who can make a whale and can make a man and make both do what He pleases."

Darrow kept Bryan on the stand for the entire

afternoon—questioning, re-questioning, asking the witness to interpret parts of the Bible. By the day's end both men were exhausted. Bryan was angry and irritable as he concluded, "The only purpose Mr. Darrow has is to slur at the Bible, but I will answer his question. . . . I want the world to know that this man, who does not believe in a God, is . . . trying to use a court in Tennessee to slur at the Bible."

"I object to your statement," Darrow interrupted. "I am examining you on your fool ideas that no intelligent Christian on earth believes."

The court banged adjournment for the day.

The next day the judge refused further testimony from Bryan. Darrow then asked that a guilty verdict be returned by the jury so the defense could appeal to the Supreme Court. The judge acceded. "Guilty," said the judge, and he set the fine at one hundred dollars.

On appeal, the Tennessee Supreme Court reversed the decision of the lower court on a technicality: the jury should have set the penalty, not the judge. The court ordered the case dismissed. No further motions were possible in the court system. Not until four decades later did the Tennessee legislature repeal the anti-evolution law.

From the start Darrow considered the Dayton case a joke, and he wanted the world to see it in this light. Dayton unwittingly cooperated with him by setting up a carnival atmosphere during the trial: hot-dog stands, popcorn stands, ice-cream vendors, evangelist tents and Holy Roller meetings, banners hanging across the streets urging "Come to Jesus," "Prepare to Meet Thy Maker." In the courtroom itself, a banner ordered, "Read Your Bible Daily."

Was Darrow too flippant, too disrespectful to religionists during the trial? Was he needlessly caustic?

If he was flippant or too biting in his satire, he was so deliberately. Was not satire Voltaire's weapon? Darrow employed shock hoping to get people to think, at least to start thinking. He too had his religion, although not in the orthodox sense. Like Thomas Paine, he believed that "to do good is my religion," and it was by this philosophy that he lived.

From the courtroom, Darrow espoused causes close to him—labor, education, social justice—and he fought against capital punishment. While he defended many black men in courtrooms, these were not cases reported widely by newspapers. The black man was a major interest of Darrow's. "I may not be true to my ideals always, but I never see a Negro without feeling that I ought to pay part of a debt to a race captured and brought here in chains," Darrow often confessed.

In Detroit, in 1926, because of the nature of the case he was defending, Clarence Darrow was given a national platform from which to plead for understanding, love, toleration, justice, equality for the black man. Dr. Ossian Sweet, a Negro and successful gynecologist who had worked under Madame Marie Curie in France on radium as it affects cancer, returned to

Detroit from Europe. He and his wife, who was a concert pianist, and their two-year-old daughter stayed with Mrs. Sweet's parents until they could find a home for themselves.

Good housing for Negroes in Detroit was hard to find. That city had become the automobile capital of the world after World War I, and it was overcrowded with workers who had come from all over the country, particularly from the South, to fill the factory jobs. In sixteen years the Negro population had increased from 6,000 to almost 70,000.

The young doctor purchased a home in a lower-middle-class white neighborhood, on the corner of Garland and Charlevoix streets in Detroit. The doctor anticipated trouble because other Negroes who had tried to move into the same neighborhood had been intimidated by the Water Works Improvement Association, formed to keep Negroes out of the area.

The day the Sweets moved into their new home a police officer was there to guard against possible violence. Helping Dr. Sweet and his wife move their possessions—which included guns, ammunition, and food—were his two brothers and several of their friends. Some white neighbors congregated before the house and remained there through the night. There was some name calling, a few stones were thrown. The next day the policeman remained on duty. Toward evening a much larger crowd, estimated to be several hundred, began to gather, and the number of police was increased.

Behind drawn shades on the second floor were the Sweets and their friends—with their guns. "I was panicked," Dr. Sweet said later. "Should we stay and fight it out? Or leave? And then what? I knew I could not leave. I owed it to my people to stay and fight for the right to stay."

The mob was getting restless; they were shrieking now and wildly throwing stones at the house. Windows shattered. Suddenly several shots were fired. A white man, part of the mob, was killed.

The eleven people in the house were arrested and charged with his murder.

A committee from the National Association for the Advancement of Colored People asked Darrow to be chief counsel in the case, and he accepted. At the trial of the eleven defendants which began in the fall of 1925, Darrow was in a more formal mood than he had been in Dayton; his famous galluses were hidden under a vest and jacket, and his gray hair was brushed back smoothly.

The defense contended that the Negroes used their constitutional rights in defending their home against anti-Negro agitation in the neighborhood and a threatening mob surrounding the house.

The State denied that any such provocation occurred. Darrow retorted that the prosecution had put enough witnesses on the stand, who said they were at the scene, to make up a mob.

As the jury could reach no verdict, it was dismissed.

In the second trial, the defense asked that each of the eleven defendants be tried separately. The first defendant was the doctor's brother, Henry Sweet, a medical student, whose trial was practically the same as the earlier one except for Darrow's final argument: "I insist that there is nothing but prejudice in this case," he told the all-white jury, "that if it was reversed and eleven white men had shot and killed a black while protecting their home and their lives against a mob of blacks, nobody would have dreamed of having them indicted. . . . There is nothing so dangerous as ignorance and bigotry when it is unleashed as it was here."

Darrow then suggested that each juror put himself in the place of the black defendants. "Make yourselves colored for a little while. It won't hurt, you can wash it off. They can't, but you can; just make yourself black for a little while; long enough, gentlemen, to judge them, and before any of you would want to be judged, you would want your juror to put himself in your place."

Again Darrow talked of love and understanding as answers to the problem of discrimination and hatred. "I would like to see a time when man loves his fellowman, and forgets his color or his creed. We will never be civilized until that time comes. . . . The law has made the Negro equal, but man has not. And, after all, the last analysis is, what has man done?—and not what has the law done?"

The jury returned a verdict of not guilty. The cases against the other defendants were dismissed.

Once more Darrow resolved to retire from the law and spend his time writing and lecturing. He wrote frequently for a number of magazines, such as *American Mercury, Vanity Fair, Collier's.* While he and Ruby were in Europe in 1928, he began to write his autobiography, *The Story of My Life*, more the philosophy of his life than the story of its activities. He debated on such subjects as "Does Man Live Again?" "Is Life Worth Living?" "Does Man Have Free Will?" always arguing the negative except when he debated "Is Civilization a Failure?" Here he answered, "Yes." But his courtroom days were not yet over. In New York he defended anti-Fascists charged with stabbing Fascists during a parade; he traveled to Rockford, Illinois, to plead for the life of a seventeen-year-old boy who was convicted of killing a streetcar conductor while drunk; in the spring of 1932 he assumed the defense of a Navy lieutenant, his mother-in-law, and two enlisted men charged with the murder of a Hawaiian who confessed to raping the Navy officer's wife.

Darrow's last major public appearance was as chairman of the review board of the National Recovery Administration. At seventy-seven years of age he conducted intensive hearings to learn whether this emergency measure of the New Deal was favoring big business over small business. The review board reported to President Franklin Roosevelt that the NRA was "tending to monopoly." Eventually the United States Supreme Court declared the NRA unconstitutional.

The lawyer's remaining years were spent serenely, reading, visiting with friends, walking in Chicago's Jackson Park with his granddaughters, often accompanied by reporters who enjoyed his cogent observations on the times.

Most of his life Clarence Darrow was a pessimist, yet he had hope. He was a hard-boiled criminal lawyer who was a sentimentalist. He fought for and defended the black man, but he had little to say about women's equality. He opposed the rugged individualism of capitalism and questioned the doctrinairism of socialism. He was a pacifist who defended World War I and then returned to his nonviolent philosophy after that war. He believed government should play a more vital role in the welfare of society, yet he resisted the growth of bureaucracy. His inconsistencies were the most consistent part of his character, except for his continuing desire to help his fellowmen. He was a free spirit not bound by tradition and orthodoxy; a perceptive and probing thinker. The issues he considered important and dealt with are still vital today—capital punishment, freedom of thought and action, civil rights, war, man's inhumanity to man.

What kind of a man was Clarence Darrow? Lincoln Steffens said it depended on the hour of the day. "At three o'clock he is a hero for courage, nerve, and calm judgment, but at three-fifteen he may be a coward for fear, collapse, and panicky mentality. A long, lean, loose body, with a heavy face that is molded like an athlete's body, he is more of a poet than a fighting attorney. He does fight; he is a great fighter as he is a good lawyer, learned and resourceful, but his power and his weakness is in the highly sensitive, emotional nature which sets his seeing mind in motion in that loafing body. His power is expression. He can say anything he wants to say, but he cannot conceal much; his face is too expressive."

Darrow died at the age of eighty-one, on March 13, 1938. His body lay in state in a funeral parlor on East 63rd Street in Chicago. Thousands came to pay their last respects. Funeral services were held in Bond Chapel at the University of Chicago. His friend Judge William Holly delivered the eulogy.

"It is a magnificent thing that Clarence Darrow lived," Judge Holly told the mourners. "In his heart was infinite pity and mercy for the poor, the oppressed, the weak and the erring—all races, all colors, all creeds, all humankind. He made the way easier for many. He preached not doctrines, but love and pity, the only virtues that can make this world any better. Thousands of lives were made easier and happier because he lived."

Darrow wanted to be cremated. His son and several of Darrow's friends scattered his ashes from the bridge dedicated in 1957 as the Clarence Darrow Memorial Bridge, during a daylong celebration honoring the centennial of his birth.

John Peter Altgeld

Courtesy Chicago Historical Society

JOHN PETER ALTGELD
1847-1902
Statesman and Democrat

ON THE MORNING of June 26, 1893, five months after his inauguration, Governor John Peter Altgeld of Illinois called his secretary into his office and told him he was going to pardon the three Haymarket anarchists. His secretary objected, saying he did not think it good policy.

The secretary's response reflected the thinking of many. The governor, however, was not interested in consensus; he was certain history would justify his pardon of the anarchists.

The Haymarket tragedy was an outgrowth of labor's militant campaign for an eight-hour workday. In Chicago, where the agitation centered, police and workers frequently battled. The city was alerted to violence, particularly for May 1, 1886, which had been proclaimed an international labor holiday dedicated to the militancy and solidarity of labor. To the surprise and relief of the power structure of the city, the day passed without major incident. On May 3, however, the police and workers clashed before the strike-bound McCormick plant. The strikers first attacked the scabs, and, in turn, the police clubbed and shot at the strikers, killing one and injuring many.

August Spies, editor of the German anarchist paper *Arbeiter Zeitung* and a militant anarchist, seeing the strikers attacked, hurried to his office and wrote what has been historically described as the "revenge" circular. It called for a meeting in Haymarket Square on May 4 to protest police brutality.

The daily press and the business community demanded suppression of the meeting, but Mayor Carter Harrison, Sr., refused to intervene. He promised to attend the meeting and, if violence threatened, to order the dispersal of the people there.

Several thousand workers gathered in the square to listen to the speakers denounce the police action at the McCormick plant. Rain began to fall, and people started to leave. The mayor stopped at the Desplaines Street police station to inform Police Captain John Bonfield that the meeting was peaceful and he could release his men from further duty. Instead of following the mayor's recommendation, the captain marched his detachment of police to Haymarket Square. As the police captain commanded the meeting immediately and peaceably to disperse, the speaker interrupted him, assuring the captain that they were peaceable. His words were cut off by the explosion of a bomb.

The police began to swing clubs and fire their guns into the fleeing crowd. It was only a matter of seconds before the Haymarket riot was over—but seven policemen were left dead and many persons were wounded.

The city was in hysteria during the weeks following the bombing. The press, the clergy, and business leaders demanded immediate action and arrests. The police put into effect a vast dragnet and arrested hundreds of labor agitators, including the feared and unpopular anarchists who were primary suspects because they were among the most active in the labor movement and took advantage of the discontent among the workers to preach their philosophy. Though anarchists advocated the "destruction of the existing class rule by all means," they also urged in their manifestos the "establishment of a free society, based upon cooperative organization of production" as well as equal rights for all "without distinction of sex or race."

Eventually eight men were accused of throwing the Haymarket bomb. No specific evidence linked these men with the act, but since some anarchists urged the use of bombs, the prosecution and the newspapers contended that the arrested anarchists were guilty.

After an eight-week trial, seven of the defendants—Albert R. Parsons, August Spies, Louis Lingg, Michael Schwab, Adolph Fischer, George Engel, and Samuel Fielden—were sentenced to hang. The eighth man, Oscar Neebe, received a fifteen-year prison term.

The public and the press approved the verdict. Anyone who questioned the conduct of the trial or the result was, in the eyes of many, an anarchist. Yet, there were doubters, among them the literary critic and writer William Dean Howells, the banker Lyman J. Gage, the brilliant orator and Republican Robert G. Ingersoll, and Altgeld's friend Clarence Darrow.

After all appeals to the higher courts, including the

United States Supreme Court, were denied, a commutation of sentence by the governor of Illinois remained the only hope to save the lives of the defendants. The day before the execution, Governor Richard Oglesby commuted the death decrees of Fielden and Schwab, who had petitioned for clemency, to life imprisonment, and on that same day Lingg committed suicide in his cell.

On November 11, 1887, Parsons, Spies, Fischer, and Engel walked to the scaffold in the Cook County jail in Chicago.

This, simply, is the Haymarket affair, but it did not end here. A gnawing doubt continued to permeate the city, the state, and the nation as an Amnesty Association, organized to plead for the pardon of the three imprisoned men, collected more than sixty thousand signatures on a petition. Both Governor Oglesby and his successor, Joseph W. Fifer, however, refused to intervene.

Altgeld, who succeeded Governor Fifer, had told his friends that if elected and if his investigation warranted it he would pardon the three Haymarket men. Two petitions faced him: one based the appeal for clemency on the fact that the men even though guilty had suffered enough; the other charged that they did not have a fair trial, that the jury was selected to convict and the judge was prejudiced.

In his "Reasons for Pardoning Fielden, Neebe, and Schwab," Altgeld set forth a definitive explanation of why he was granting an absolute pardon. He contended that if the defendants had a fair trial and if there was no new evidence to show that they were innocent of the crime, "then there ought to be no executive interference, for no punishment under our laws could be too severe. Government must defend itself; life and property must be protected, and law and order must be maintained." Then he turned to the second petition and began to discuss the ways the police department had produced evidence. He cited an interview with a police captain in which the captain said he tried to calm matters after the Haymarket bomb throwing, but another captain wanted to keep things stirring, wanted bombs to be found everywhere. After the anarchist groups were broken up, this captain wanted to send men out to organize new anarchist societies right away to "keep himself prominent before the public."

Regarding the record of the trial, Altgeld believed it showed that the jury "in this case was not drawn in the manner that juries usually are drawn; that, instead of having a number of names drawn out of a box that contained many hundreds of names, as the law contemplates shall be done . . . the trial judge appointed . . . a special bailiff to go out and summon such men as he [the bailiff] might select to act as jurors."

He cited specific instances of questioning of prospective jurors by the prosecuting attorney and the judge, which indicated an attempt to get prejudiced jurors. A dry goods merchant, for example, said he had formed an opinion about the guilt of the defendants. He admitted, when challenged by the court, that his prejudice would handicap him, to which the judge had observed, "Well, that is sufficient qualification for a juror in the case; of course, the more a man feels that he is handicapped the more he will be guarded against it."

Altgeld further noted in his pardon message that the state never found who threw the bomb that killed the policemen, and there was no evidence linking the defendants with the man who did throw it.

In his conclusion, Altgeld pointed out that while some of the charges against the judge during the Haymarket trial were of a personal character, these seemed to be warranted by the record of the trial. The trial was not fair, Altgeld stressed, and therefore it was his duty to grant an absolute pardon to Neebe, Fielden, and Schwab.

The opposition Governor Altgeld had anticipated would follow his act came immediately. "Demagogue," "foreigner," "Un-American," "apologist for murder," "anarchist," "encourager of lawlessness," "champion of anarchy," shouted the press, and the public.

The New York *Sun* used poetry on its editorial page to express its feelings about Altgeld and his action:

O, Wild Chicago, When the Time
Is Ripe for Ruin's deeds,
When constitutions, courts, and laws
Go down midst crashing creeds,

John Peter Altgeld

Lift up your weak and guilty hands
From out the wreck of states
And as the crumbling towers fall down
Write ALTGELD on your gates!

Even among those who wanted the Haymarket anarchists freed and who lauded Altgeld's action were many who believed the governor had criticized the judge too severely. "Governor Altgeld was wrong in laying all the blame on the judge," said Clarence Darrow. Jane Addams of Hull-House believed that "a magnanimous action was marred by personal rancor, betraying for the moment the infirmity of a noble mind."

The New York *World*, on June 27, 1893, probably summarized the feeling of most people by writing, "It is not the fact that these men have been given their liberty that is remarkable and startling. It is the tone of Governor Altgeld's statement in which he sets forth the reasons for the action that will astonish if it does not alarm the country."

Altgeld, however, felt strongly about his reasons for the pardon, and he could not soften them. This was not to be the only time he did not consider public opinion. In the years to come he would attract national attention many times as he openly criticized injustices and sought social reforms.

John Peter Altgeld, the first foreign-born governor of Illinois, was born in Germany on December 30, 1847, and brought to the United States shortly afterward. His parents, John and Mary Lanehart Altgeld, settled in a small German community in the village of Newville in Richland County, near Mansfield, Ohio, where the elder Altgeld became a farmer. The life was hard and frugal. John Peter helped to plow the field and peddle farm products to other homes in the small settlement. At fourteen he went to work for a neighboring farmer, contributing all his earnings to his family.

The young boy dreamed of other things besides farm work. He yearned for education and the world into which it would lead him. Despite the hardships, he managed to attend a district school for several winter terms and then a German parish school for more than a year. He studied the German Bible and the few other German books he found in his own home, and he diligently read the books of history, biography, poetry, philosophy, and theology that he found in neighbors' homes.

His father thought education useless and resented his son's desire to learn. A strict, hardheaded disciplinarian, he was not above using a horsewhip on John Peter and the five younger children to instill obedience to the household rules. The mother was a kindhearted woman who loved her children but neither understood nor sympathized with her oldest son's dreams.

The Civil War broke out when Altgeld was thirteen years old. The Ohio National Guard recruited a regiment in Richland County, and the young boy's patriotism was aroused as he watched the drilling. When President Lincoln asked for additional troops early in 1864, the governor of Ohio suggested that the state militia answer the President's call. Sixteen-year-old John Peter enlisted as a substitute for one of the regular militiamen who did not want to go. Of the one hundred dollars he was paid for enlisting, Altgeld gave ninety dollars to his father to make up for not working on the farm.

John Peter Altgeld's regiment fought at Richmond where General Grant defeated General Lee; it participated in skirmishes along the Petersburg and Richmond Railway. At Wilson's Landing it built entrenchments, went on reconnaissance patrols, and later helped build Fort Pocahontas. Little is known of what part Altgeld played in these events. At Wilson's Landing he became ill with a fever, spent time in a field hospital, and was mustered out with the regiment in the fall of 1864.

Altgeld rarely spoke of his war experience. When he accepted the nomination for governor of Illinois, he modestly covered this episode in his life by saying, "Your candidate for Governor . . . when sixteen years old, went into the Union army, and for some months carried a gun around in the swamps below Richmond. He did not bleed and did not die, but was there; always reported for duty, always on deck, never shirked and never ran away."

During the uproar which followed his pardoning of the Haymarket anarchists, Altgeld's friends pleaded with him to talk of his boyhood service in the Union army in answer to the charges being hurled against him.

"My war experience is nothing of consequence," was his reply. "I was a boy then, and merely did what most of the other boys were doing. It was the enthusiasm of those days, the drums and flags and all the rest of it, that led me to enlist. Neither then nor since did I look upon myself as a hero for having gone into the army. And as a matter of fact, not all that I went through in the war required half the courage that it took to sign the anarchist pardons."

When he returned from the war, Altgeld again went to work on the family farm, but now he was even more dissatisfied with farm life than before; he had seen a wider world and he was eager to take part in it. Furthermore, the fever had weakened him and he was not able to do all the physical work the farm required.

Despite the obstacles placed in his path by his father, young Altgeld did attend a private school briefly, after which he began to teach school and to study law at night. But to keep peace in the family, the son set aside his ambition for a while and continued to work in the fields until he was twenty-one and legally able to make his own decisions. Then he left Newville, wandered from Cincinnati to East St. Louis, walking most of the way, stopping occasionally to work for a meal or a night's lodging. He worked with pick and shovel as a railroad laborer. He did odd jobs as he traveled across Missouri, eventually settling in Savannah, Missouri, where he again taught school, worked on a farm, and studied law with a lawyer. In 1871 he was admitted to the bar.

John Peter Altgeld began his law practice in Savannah where, after several years, he was elected prosecuting attorney. He soon realized, however, that the system of which he had become a part was "a great mill which, in one way or another, supplies its own grist; a maelstrom which draws from the outside and then keeps its victims moving in a circle until swallowed in the vortex." After serving half of his two-year term of office he resigned, sold his law books for one hundred dollars, and headed for Chicago.

The vigor of the young city, actively rebuilding itself from the fire which had practically leveled it four years earlier, appealed to him. In Chicago, the twenty-eight-year-old lawyer rented office space in the newly constructed Reaper Block building in the city's downtown area. Edward Osgood Brown, a lawyer on the same floor of the building, recalled his first meeting with Altgeld, who came to his office one morning asking "for the loan of some trifling object." The young lawyer had rented the room down the hall and was going to partition off part of it for sleeping quarters so that he could live as well as do business in his office. Brown, who later became a close friend to Altgeld, said Altgeld "was not, as such things are superficially considered, an attractive or graceful personality, and yet there was something about him that instantly arrested our attention and invited our respect and friendship."

Altgeld worked on some lawsuits for Brown and his

partner. They were impressed with the young lawyer's conscientiousness, his exacting and meticulous research. Altgeld one day complained to Brown about the slow progress he was making in the preparation of some legal papers, saying that he had to look at the dictionary for one word in every five to know that he had spelled it right. Such tenacity characterized Altgeld as he mastered the English language, became an authority on the law and an effective public speaker, even writing a book on *Oratory.*

While visiting his parents in Ohio in 1877, Altgeld remet his teen-age sweetheart whose father, some years earlier, had refused to allow her to marry the penniless young man. Their romance was renewed, and they were married in November of that year. A college graduate and a schoolteacher, Emma Ford Altgeld was completely devoted to her husband and influenced him by her refinement and sensitivity. Except for the fact that they had no children, the marriage was exceedingly happy.

Chicago was good to the young lawyer. He prospered both in his law practice and in his real estate investments, where he demonstrated an unusual acumen. He had great faith in the future of the city, and his analysis of the land transactions in which he engaged was almost always accurate. By 1890 he was reputed to have amassed a million dollars.

Altgeld planned to build the finest office building in the world, and blueprints were drawn for the Unity Building, a sixteen-story fireproof structure in Chicago's Loop. When friends questioned the risk he was taking with his personal fortune, Altgeld replied that since he was childless he looked upon his buildings as children which would survive him and benefit the generations to come. To Jane Addams he commented once that the Unity Building had given him his greatest personal satisfaction.

Altgeld eventually lost the Unity Building, however, because of construction problems, the economic depression of 1893, and other financial troubles with which he had not reckoned when he first proposed the skyscraper. Had he considered only himself, this dream of his would have ended differently. He could have saved his personal fortune if, later as governor, he had signed the "eternal monopoly bills" giving Charles T. Yerkes, art connoisseur and financial titan, a long-term franchise on the street and elevated railways in Chicago. There was at least a half-million dollars waiting for the governor, it was indicated to him. Money had already been used to get the bill through the legislature, and all the governor had to do was to accept the bribe and sign the bill.

But Altgeld, uncompromising in his honesty, believed the Yerkes monopoly wrong for the public, and he vetoed the bill. The legislature did not have enough votes to override his veto, and when the Unity Building was forced to default on interest on its bonds, the financial forces which could have saved him turned away because of that veto.

During his early political career, Altgeld was elected

judge of the Superior Court of Cook County, and ultimately his associate judges named him chief justice. However, again he became restless; the position was too much a part of "the system," too confining. He resigned before his term expired.

He continued to read, to study the social problems of the day. In 1884 he published a 151-page book entitled *Our Penal Machinery and Its Victims*. The volume represented Altgeld's reflections on crime, prison institutions, and their inhabitants. It had a profound influence on his future friend, Clarence Darrow, at this time a practicing attorney in Ashtabula, Ohio.

In his book Altgeld posed various questions. Does the prison system as it now stands make criminals out of many who are not naturally so? Is it not virtually impossible for those once committed to prison to be anything else but criminals? Can the prison system repress those who do not want to be anything but criminals?

Altgeld challenged the prevailing views of the orthodox criminologists of his day. He insisted that history could not point to a single instance where punishment and cruelty effected a genuine reformation. "It can crush," he pointed out, "but it cannot improve. It can restrain, but as soon as the restraint is removed the subject is worse than before. The human mind is so constituted that it must be led toward the good, and can be driven only in one direction, and that is toward ruin."

Altgeld asserted that "the multitude of first offenders comes from the weaker class." He argued, "They should be treated rather as wards, whom it may be necessary to confine, but whom it is yet necessary to train and educate, if possible, into good citizens."

He further urged that the prisoner "be not only permitted, but required, to earn something for himself while in prison, over and above the actual expense of keeping him." He suggested the concept—still considered radical today—of indeterminate sentences in which the length of a prisoner's confinement would be determined by his conduct, with a board of governors deciding whether the prisoner should be returned to society.

Altgeld wrote prolifically during the 1880's for magazines and newspapers on a variety of subjects, ranging from arbitration of strikes and police brutality to justice as administered in Chicago, immigrant problems, and the eight-hour workday.

In 1892 the Democratic machine in Illinois needed the German vote. Altgeld was of German descent, which was an asset in the political arena in that particular election. The previous Republican legislature had offended both Catholics and Lutherans by passing the "little red school house" legislation, a compulsory school law which required that all classes be held in English and be subject to inspection by state truant officers.

In addition to his German extraction, Altgeld fitted the requisites for the Democratic nominee for governor. He was known as a friend of the poor and of the laboring man, he had been a judge, he was ambitious and wealthy and could make a substantial contribution to the campaign fund. He became a familiar figure—his hair worn in a crew cut, his beard neatly trimmed to hide a harelip—as he campaigned across the state for the Democratic national ticket headed by Grover Cleveland for President and himself as governor of Illinois. The slate was victorious: Cleveland was elected President, and Illinois, for the first time in thirty-six years, had a Democratic governor.

Immediately after his inauguration Altgeld was besieged with petitions requesting a pardon for the Chicago anarchists involved in the Haymarket affair. Five months later he acted. The imprisoned men were freed, the dead exonerated—and the storm broke that was to harass Altgeld through his four-year term. Almost everything he did after that was labeled "anarchist."

Two years after Altgeld's pardon action, Eugene Victor Debs led the American Railway Union in a strike against the railroads (see Debs, pp. 67 ff.). A special assistant federal district attorney convinced President Cleveland to send troops into Illinois to protect the city from rioters because the "anarchist" Altgeld was encouraging the mob and cooperating with it. Immediately Altgeld became embroiled in a controversy with the President.

Learning of the federal troops in Chicago, Governor Altgeld wrote to President Cleveland on July 5, 1894: "Sir: I am advised that you have ordered Federal troops to go into service in the State of Illinois. Surely the facts have not been correctly presented to you in this case, or you would not have taken this step, for it is entirely unnecessary, and, as it seems to me, unjustifiable.

"Waiving all questions of courtesy," the governor continued, "I will say that the State of Illinois is not only able to take care of itself, but it stands ready to furnish the Federal government any assistance it may need elsewhere. Our military force is ample, and consists of as good soldiers as can be found in the country." Furthermore, he had been advised that the local officials had the situation under control.

To prove his contention, Altgeld related instances where the United States marshal for the southern district of Illinois applied for assistance to help enforce a federal court order, and state troops were promptly furnished. He also told of sending state troops to railroad centers when requested by local authorities. The governor said that newspaper stories had exaggerated the violence of the ARU strike, and he asked for the immediate withdrawal of the troops.

President Cleveland retorted that "Federal troops were sent to Chicago in strict accordance with the Constitution and laws of the United States, upon the demand of the post-office department that obstruction of the mails should be removed, and upon the representations of the judicial officers of the United States that the process of the Federal courts could not be executed through the ordinary means, and upon competent proof that conspiracies existed against commerce between the States."

The governor was not satisfied, and in another dispatch to the President he again demanded the withdrawal of the federal troops. But the President replied that it would be better if "in this hour of danger and public distress, discussion [gave] way to active efforts on the part of all in authority to restore obedience to law and to protect life and property."

Again the press began to attack the governor. Again they called him a "defender of lawlessness," a "champion of anarchy." Godwin's conservative *Nation* agreed with the President's "method of dealing with Governor Altgeld" and referred to it as "a model one."

In reviewing the Pullman case at a meeting in Cooper Union, New York, in the fall of 1896, Altgeld coined the phrase "government by injunction." He claimed that the federal courts had "established a form of government that is government by injunction, under which the federal judge becomes at once legislator, judge, and executioner. Sitting in his chambers and without notice to anybody he issues a ukase, which he calls an injunction, against all people of a State, forbidding anything he sees fit to forbid and which the law does not forbid, for when the law forbids a thing there is no need of an injunction.

"By this injunction," Altgeld explained, "the judge can forbid anything which whim, prejudice, or caprice may suggest, and his order is law and must stand until it is reversed by a superior authority."

Altgeld's indictment of government by injunction was the antecedent to the Norris-LaGuardia Act passed in 1932, which restricted the use of injunctions in labor disputes.

Though the most dramatic and most publicized events in Governor Altgeld's term in office were the Haymarket pardons and the controversy with President Cleveland, there were other moments of greatness in the career of this man who was so mercilessly decried by the Establishment of his day.

It was Altgeld, as governor of Illinois, who initiated various legislative bills for social reform, among them prison reform, including a parole system in the state and the construction of a state reformatory for girls.

It was Altgeld who enforced the state's child labor law. Up until he was elected governor, the law which forbade children under thirteen years of age to work in factories and stores only adorned the state books. He named Florence Kelly of Hull-House as state factory inspector. Miss Kelly enforced the law so effectively that a prominent Illinois businessman threatened to close his factory and nail a sign to the door: "Closed because of the pernicious legislation in Illinois." Altgeld suggested a more appropriate legend would be: "Closed in the interest of the children of Illinois."

It was Altgeld who raised the status of the University of Illinois from a technical school, teaching agriculture and mechanical arts, to a great school of learning. He expanded its curricula, planned more buildings, added more teachers, and increased student enrollment.

To have good schools, Altgeld reasoned, there must be competent teachers, and so the governor, called by his enemies "the fomenter of anarchy," secured the passage of bills which established a normal college for teachers in DeKalb and another at Charleston, Illinois.

"While a college education is invaluable," the governor told the University of Illinois graduating class in 1893, "it is not the end and aim of life. . . . Education means training, not memorizing or stuffing. The mind must be a workshop, not a storehouse."

Over his objections, Altgeld was renominated for governor by the Democratic party in 1896. That same year he led the Illinois delegation to the Democratic national convention, where he was a dominant figure, shaping the party platform and instrumental in the nomination of William Jennings Bryan for President. Had Altgeld been native born he undoubtedly would have been chosen the party's standard bearer at this convention. When Altgeld was complimented on his influence in the convention proceedings, he commented with a smile: "Yes, I did everything but nominate myself; that was prevented by an accident of birth and a clause in the constitution." Bryan and Altgeld were both defeated; it was a Republican year.

In Illinois, custom called for the retiring executive to speak at the inauguration ceremony of his successor. So bitter was the acrimony of Altgeld's victorious Republican opponent that the governor-elect withheld this traditional courtesy from Altgeld, who had prepared a farewell address and distributed advance copies to the newspapers. Altgeld was not told until the last minute, after the press had the speech, that he would not be permitted to speak. The next morning the papers carried the undelivered speech, which read in part:

"I have tried to further the best interests of my country, and while I erred in many cases they were errors of judgment and I go forth with a peaceful conscience. I have endeavored to carry out those principles that form the basis of free government, and I have acted on the conviction that it would be better to be Governor but for one day and follow the dictates of justice than to hold office for fifty years by winking at wrong. In my judgment no epitaph can be written upon the tomb of a public man that will so surely win the contempt of the ages than to say of him that he held office all his life and never did anything for humanity."

The ex-governor, nevertheless, continued to participate in Democratic politics. He campaigned for Carter H. Harrison, Jr., in Harrison's successful bid for mayor of Chicago in 1897 and despaired when the newly elected mayor joined forces with Altgeld's enemies, even naming several to key jobs in his administration. Furthermore, there were indications that Harrison was aligning himself with New York's Tammany Hall boss, Richard Crocker, in a move to control the 1900 Democratic national convention and defeat the free silver platform passed at the 1896 convention.

Altgeld's friends convinced him to oppose Harrison at the next mayoral election in 1899 on an independent ticket. He agreed, although he lacked both the finances and the physical energy to carry on a strong campaign. He explained his defection from the Democratic party by saying, "To worship a corrupt political organization as a fetish, and blindly follow it when it is moving toward destruction, is unworthy of a free citizen; and this practice has done infinite harm to our republic. Political machinery is a curse when prostituted to base purposes." When the votes were counted, Altgeld was third in a three-way race.

After his defeat and Harrison's control of the Illinois Democratic organization, Altgeld attended the 1900 Democratic convention as a private member of the party. The convention, however, reaffirmed the 1896 platform, nominated Bryan again for the presidency, and adopted an Altgeld-sponsored plank that imperialism was the "paramount issue of the campaign." This issue of imperialism was an outgrowth of the Spanish-American War. As a result of Spain's defeat, the Philippines were transferred from Spain to the United States without the consent of the Filipinos, who had expected they would be given immediate independence. The Altgeld forces objected to territorial expansion without the consent of the people involved, which they labeled "imperialism." Altgeld helped direct the Bryan forces and traveled with the Presidential candidate in his swing through the New England states. The country, however, did not want change; prosperity and the "full dinner pail" were more important to it than anti-imperialism or free silver. The Republican victory was even more sweeping than in 1896.

At fifty-three, in ill health, out of Democratic party politics, Altgeld was a disappointed man. The fires of ambition, both in politics and business, were gone. He opened a law office, but at the insistence of his friend Clarence Darrow he joined the firm of Darrow and Thompson. The name of the partnership was changed to Altgeld, Darrow, and Thompson, with Altgeld the senior partner.

On March 11, 1902, Altgeld spent most of the morning in federal court arguing the case of a local cabmen's union against a railroad. In the afternoon he boarded a train for Joliet, where he spoke at a mass meeting protesting Great Britain's treatment of the Boers and demanding independence for this large segment of South Africa's population. He began his Joliet speech with vigor. Several times during his talk he leaned on the table to keep from falling, yet he continued to speak. He concluded: "I am not discouraged. Things will right themselves. The pendulum swings one way and then another. But the steady pull of gravitation is toward the center of the earth. Any structure must be plumb if it is to endure, or the building will fall. So it is with nations. Wrong may seem to triumph. Right may seem to be defeated.

But the gravitation of eternal justice is toward the Throne of God. Any political institution which is to endure must be plumb with that line of justice."

Those were the last words he spoke in public. He acknowledged the applause, began to walk off the stage, staggered, and just as he reached the wings he fell.

He was taken to his hotel room in a semiconscious condition. He gained consciousness long enough to express concern for his wife who was in frail health and whom he did not want to alarm. "I've got to be careful of her, you know," he said.

Shortly afterward he became unconscious. Early Wednesday morning, March 12, 1902, the twentieth governor of Illinois died in his hotel room in Joliet.

A bereaved Clarence Darrow came to take the body of his associate to Chicago. First there were private services in Altgeld's home where a clergyman officiated and Jane Addams and Darrow eulogized their friend.

The governor of Illinois offered a military escort to accompany the casket from Altgeld's home to the Chicago Public Library where it lay in state, and from the library to the cemetery. Mrs. Altgeld declined the offer. A newspaper headline announced:

"Pomp of War Not to Mark Funeral."

At the library—from eleven o'clock in the morning to ten at night—and all the next morning—from forty to fifty thousand admirers slowly passed the coffin. Most had to stand in the rain on a cold day waiting to get one last look at the man who sacrificed his career for his belief in justice.

After the doors were closed to the public, William Jennings Bryan spoke at the bier: "All of us who knew him can be glad of this, that his last blows were struck in the cause of an oppressed people, in a cause to which he was devoted."

At his death, even the Chicago *Tribune*, his most bitter critic, observed: "The hatred of his opponents was a tribute to his ability. None but a strong man could have worked his way up to national prominence as Mr. Altgeld did. . . . Men went to listen to him because he was a man exceedingly in earnest, saying things which were unpleasant often, but which were known to be the genuine sentiments of the speaker."

John Peter Altgeld carried the weight of mankind on his shoulders as he viewed the world through sad eyes. Courageous, philosophical, and unafraid to stand alone, he hated injustice, whether to himself or to others. Impatient at obstacles, he yet had the patience to bide his time to overcome them. He had a logical, orderly mind which enabled him to deal calmly and reflectively with problems that aroused emotionalism on the part of the public and the press. He loved books, music, and poetry, but he loved the outdoors, too, and was a superb horseman.

Though Vachel Lindsey in his powerful poem about Altgeld, published in 1912, called the governor "an eagle forgotten," today Altgeld's name is synonymous with the best and the most courageous of American political idealism.

Jane Addams

Courtesy Jane Addams Memorial Collection, University of Illinois, Chicago

JANE ADDAMS

1860-1935

Social Worker and World Citizen

"FOR YEARS," recalled a former resident of Hull-House, one of the first social settlements in the United States, "Jane Addams and Clarence Darrow were in a tug of war for young souls like mine."

Darrow delighted in teasing the young settlement workers. He would ask, "What are you doing at Hull-House?" To which a resident once responded seriously that she helped to furnish "legitimate amusement for the people."

Darrow laughed. "Is that the kind of entertainment they want?"

Hull-House, however, did more than provide "legitimate amusement for the people." Hull-House, as personified by Jane Addams, was a social conscience, a harbinger of hopes and aspirations not only for the immediate neighborhood which it served but for all men, women, and children in search of a better life.

According to its charter, Hull-House set out "to provide a center for a higher civic and social life; to institute and maintain educational and philanthropic enterprises, and to investigate and improve the conditions in the industrial districts of Chicago." This is what it did—and what it continues to do today.

At the age of seven, Jane Addams, founder of Hull-House, saw poverty for the first time, and she was deeply impressed with the demoralizing effect it had on its victims. She had accompanied her father on a business trip to Freeport, Illinois, a neighboring town somewhat larger than her native Cedarville. She had been there many times before and always found it a fascinating and exciting city with its toy shop and candy store. This time, however, Mr. Addams visited a mill located in the poorest part of the city. To the young Jane the contrast "between the ruddy poverty of the country and that which even a small city presents in its shabbiest streets" was overwhelming.

"Why do people live in such horrid little houses so close together?" she cried.

Her father explained that many people did not have enough money to live in nicer places.

"Well," the child declared firmly, "when I grow up I shall have a large house, but it won't be built near other large houses but right in the midst of horrid little houses like these."

The little girl who made this prophetic declaration was born in Cedarville, Illinois, on September 6, 1860. She was the youngest of eight children of whom only four lived to maturity. Her father, John Addams, a successful miller, was a foe of slavery, actively aiding runaway slaves in their flight to freedom. His home was a station in the underground railroad. During the Civil War he helped to form and equip a company of soldiers known as the Addams Guard, and for sixteen years—throughout the war and the years following—

he was a member of the Illinois legislature where he became a friend of Abraham Lincoln. Years later his daughter reminisced about the letters her father received from Mr. Lincoln when they were both members of the legislature. The letters always began, "My dear Double-d'ed Addams."

From her Quaker father, Jane Addams inherited a sense of obligation toward her fellowmen which remained with her throughout her life. She adored her father; she considered him the wisest, the most just of all men, and she took pride in his handsome appearance. She was very conscious of her slight deformity caused by a spinal curvature, and when strangers were nearby she would not walk along the street with her father because she did not want anyone to know that the "ugly pigeon-toed little girl," as she was later to describe herself, "whose crooked back obliged her to walk with her head held very much upon one side," was the "daughter of this fine gentleman."

Sarah Addams, Jane's mother, died when Jane was two years old. Six years later her father married a Freeport widow, Anna Haldeman, a high-spirited, wealthy, and talented woman. The new wife, whom Jane respected and admired, brought with her to the Addams home her younger son, seven-year-old George Haldeman, and he and the young Jane became inseparable friends until they both went away to college. In later years he wanted to marry her, although he never understood her "philanthropic nonsense."

With her education in the Cedarville school system

completed, Jane Addams wanted to attend Smith College in the East. Instead, she followed family tradition and enrolled in nearby Rockford Female Seminary from which her sisters had graduated and where her father was a trustee. At the seminary she wrote for the school magazine and was its editor-in-chief in her senior year, when she also was elected class president and named valedictorian of the class of 1881.

Two months after her graduation from Rockford, Jane's father died. He was widely known and highly respected in the community. His death deeply depressed Jane Addams and left her in a state of confusion regarding her future. She wrote to her friend Ellen Gates Starr, who later helped her to found Hull-House, "The greatest sorrow that can ever come has passed and I hope it is only a question of time until I get my moral purposes straightened."

She enrolled at the Woman's Medical College at Philadelphia, but she had barely started her studies when her spinal condition began to bother her. Surgery was performed to correct the curvature, and for six months she was bedridden. When her health improved, Jane went to Europe with her stepmother. They traveled for two years, visiting Dublin, London, Berlin, Amsterdam, Dresden—where she studied German—Italy, Venice, and Paris. They toured art galleries, attended concerts and the opera, but Jane was restless and impatient. Having given up the idea of a career in medicine because of her health, she was searching for a purpose to her life. Still in the back of her mind was the childhood dream of helping to improve conditions for poor people.

From Europe she went with Mrs. Addams to Baltimore where they visited George Haldeman, her stepbrother, who was doing graduate work at Johns Hopkins University. Her stepmother, recalling the affection between the two in earlier years, hoped that this visit might bring them to marriage. Instead, it made Jane only more nervous and depressed.

A second trip to Europe, this time with some college friends including Ellen Gates Starr, was more rewarding for the twenty-seven-year-old Miss Addams. The trip started with the usual cycle of concerts, galleries, operas, and study. But a bullfight in Spain, which the group attended, awakened Jane Addams to the fact that she was just biding her time and not making any contribution to society. The shock to her lethargy came when she realized she was the only one of her group who had stayed to the end of the bullfight program in which five bulls and a number of horses were killed.

"How could you!" her friends reproached her when they later met in the lobby of their hotel. "How could you have such brutal endurance!"

She offered them no defense, but she later wrote that "the natural and inevitable reaction came" in the evening and "I felt myself tried and condemned, not only by this disgusting experience but by the entire moral situation which it revealed."

The bullfight incident propelled Jane Addams into

action. For the first time she confided to Ellen Starr her dream of a "large house near horrid little houses" and asked her friend to join her in making it come true. Miss Starr enthusiastically accepted the idea, and together they started their plans.

Before returning to the United States, Jane Addams journeyed to London where she spent six weeks in that city's slums. She visited Toynbee Hall, founded in 1884, the first settlement house ever established, where university men lived and worked among the poor, participating in the clubs, classes, and the other cultural activities offered.

In January 1889 Jane Addams and Ellen Starr came to Chicago to search for a house that would be suitable for their settlement. While traveling around the poorer sections of the city, Miss Addams spotted an old house on Halsted Street south of Polk Street, made of brick with a veranda on three sides and wooden pillars of Corinthian design framing the entrance. The gracious-looking building had been built in 1856 on what were then the outskirts of Chicago by Charles J. Hull, a successful real estate man. After his wife and children died, he willed the home and his estate of more than four million dollars to his cousin and secretary, Helen Culver. Now, thirty-three years after the house was built, the city had grown around it, and it stood surrounded by tenements.

The house was rented as an office and storeroom when the two friends first saw it. After some negotiating they were able to sublet the second floor and part of the first floor. Immediately they began to repair cracked ceilings, polish the wood panelings and oak floors, and restore the marble fireplaces. They furnished the house with horsehair, mahogany, and walnut furniture of the period, and lovingly placed their own few pieces of porcelain collected during their European trips.

Before long, Miss Culver, Mr. Hull's cousin, became interested in the social settlement and offered the house rent-free to the social workers. Eventually both the house and land were deeded to Hull-House, which in time expanded to thirteen buildings—all built upon Mr. Hull's land.

When Hull-House opened its doors on September 18, 1889, the neighborhood was a conglomerate of immigrant colonies of Italians, Germans—including German Jews—Polish and Russian Jews, Bohemians, Irish, and first-generation Americans. Immediately surrounding Hull-House were mostly frame houses originally built as one-family units but now occupied by several families.

The first residents of Hull-House were Jane Addams, Ellen Starr, and Mary Keyser, who originally came to do the housework but soon became an integral part of the settlement house projects.

The response from the outside community was enthusiastic. Ellen Starr, vivacious, intense, stimulated by the idea of instilling a love of the beautiful in everyone, had been an art instructor in a fashionable private school and knew many people of affluence in the city. To them, she and Jane Addams explained their purpose which, simply stated, was to help the neighbors. The two social workers also found a sympathetic response from ministers, women's clubs, philanthropists, and newspapers. There were many volunteers.

The neighbors, on the other hand, eyed the three Hull-House women suspiciously. Why would rich ladies come to live in the squalor of a foreign slum? they wondered. They soon learned that the ladies asked for nothing except to share what they had with the poor. Hull-House doors were always open. At first some of the neighboring women came just to see, but they came back with others, again and again, for at Hull-House they found warmth and friendship; people who cared and understood one's problems, who were ready to listen and to help. Here adults and children could play and learn, as there were classes in English, music, painting, drama, crafts.

The activities at Hull-House evolved gradually. A series of readings directed by Ellen Starr was one of the first of the planned programs, with George Eliot's *Romola* the first book read. There were parallels between the humanitarian services of the novel's heroine in a small Italian village and that of Jane Addams and Ellen Starr in the Hull-House area.

From the start, Hull-House was prepared to perform a variety of services. Many hours were spent to get "support for deserted women, insurance for bewildered widows, damages for injured operators, furniture from the clutches of the installment store." There was the November evening a fifteen-year-old Italian bride came to the house seeking shelter. Her husband had beaten her every night for a week because she had lost her wedding ring. There was another night when Miss Addams and another Hull-House resident, Julia Lathrop—who was later active in the organization of the Cook County Juvenile Court—acted as midwives to deliver an illegitimate baby because "the doctor was late in arriving, and none of the Irish matrons would 'touch the likes of her.' "

Afterward, Miss Addams commented: "This doing things that we don't know how to do is going too far. Why did we let ourselves be rushed into midwifery?"

But Julia Lathrop defined the meaning of Hull-House with her answer: "If we have to begin to hew down to the line of our ignorance, for goodness' sake don't let us begin at the humanitarian end! If Hull-House doesn't have its roots in human kindness, it is no good at all."

A major problem in the Hull-House neighborhood was poor sanitary conditions in the alleys. The sporadic garbage collections made the area particularly unhealthy and dangerous because of the large amounts of decayed fruit and vegetables thrown out by the Italian and Greek peddlers who lived there. Added to this were the disease-ridden piles of filthy rags which the rag pickers would pull out of the city dumps and bring home for further sorting and washing. Sickening odors came from the wooden boxes in the alleys. These conditions led to many deaths each year.

To help relieve the situation, talks on sanitation

were arranged for the immigrants. The housewife was told she must keep not only her own house clean but also the streets. Though in her native village she might sweep the refuse into the street and then let it decay in the open air, this was not healthy in the crowded quarters in which she now lived.

Jane Addams became particularly aware of the sanitation problem in her area when her nephew, for whom she had been appointed guardian, could not come to live with her at Hull-House. The doctor judged that he was too delicate and would die in the unsanitary environment. Ashamed that she had done nothing about the garbage situation earlier, before it had become her personal problem, she and the residents of the settlement house began to inquire into the methods used in the collection of garbage. Within two months, they discovered 1,037 violations overlooked by the city inspectors. The city's health department was alerted, and, as a result, three city garbage inspectors were transferred to other areas. The unsanitary conditions, however—and the garbage—remained.

The following spring, in an attempt to get a more efficient collection of refuse, Miss Addams bid for the garbage removal service contract. Although her bid was rejected on a technicality, the publicity prompted the mayor of Chicago to appoint her garbage inspector for the ward. She in turn named as deputy a young lady, a University of Wisconsin graduate who had done similar work both in Pittsburgh and Chicago;

and for the next three years, the last two of which were under civil service, the deputy successfully fulfilled her inspection duties. Eventually, because of a political power play, the alderman eliminated the job by introducing a new civil service position of ward superintendent, specifically designated as a man's job.

Among the activities at Hull-House were the meetings held by the fledgling labor unions. Jane Addams encouraged labor organizations in their struggles against long hours, unsafe working conditions, and the sweatshops of the garment industry. Since Chicago was a center of the garment trades and many of the workers in the industry lived around Hull-House, the cloakmakers and the shirtmakers organized their unions at the settlement.

Jane Addams, the practical idealist, acted—sometimes successfully, sometimes unsuccessfully—as an arbitrator in labor-management disputes. She was a member of the Citizens' Arbitration Committee named during the Pullman strike, an event which brought Eugene Victor Debs, Clarence Darrow, and Governor John Peter Altgeld of Illinois to national prominence. She knew George M. Pullman and the pride he felt in the model town he had built for his employees on the southern outskirts of Chicago, but she also knew Pullman, Illinois, as a town dominated, governed, and owned by George Pullman. The Citizens' Arbitration Committee failed in its efforts to arbitrate the issues between the Pullman company and the American Railway Union during the strike.

Even though Miss Addams was merely an appointed arbitrator in this strike, as she was to be later in the 1905 teamster strike, she and Hull-House were criticized, and both lost friends. But she insisted that the settlement's demands for social justice and social order committed it to an effort to understand and, as far as possible, to alleviate the pressures brought about by the industrial system.

In their investigation of the poverty of the neighborhood, Hull-House residents found sweatshops where women sewed for twelve to fourteen hours a day. They had little or no time to care for their children, who in many instances were left with neighbors already overburdened with the care of their own children. Sometimes youngsters were left alone, locked in a room in their tenement apartment. To fill the need for child care for working mothers, Hull-House opened a day nursery.

Young children themselves worked long hours in factories. The tragedy of child labor was poignantly emphasized to Jane Addams and her co-workers at the settlement's carefully planned first Christmas party in 1889 when some of the very young children refused candy, pleading, "Oh, please take it away. We work in a candy factory, and we can't stand to look at candy." Upon further inquiry, the social workers learned that for six weeks prior to the holiday many of the children had been working in a candy factory from seven in the morning to nine at night.

That same winter Jane Addams became acquainted

with the pledges signed by parents of children working in factories, which promised that the parents would make no claim for damages resulting from "carelessness" at work. Three boys from a Hull-House club were injured at a machine in a neighboring factory. One of the boys died. The machine needed only an inexpensive protective guard to avoid such accidents, but the manufacturer refused to provide this. "We were sure the owners would in some way do something to help the families as well as to prevent similar tragedies in the future. To our surprise, they did nothing," Miss Addams commented dejectedly.

In an effort to abolish some of these problems, Hull-House lobbied for labor legislation, including an eight-hour workday law for women. Out of the experiences and activities of the Hull-House residents, the first juvenile court was set up in Chicago, the city's first public playground was built, and public baths were opened because such facilities were missing in most tenement apartments in the area.

Much of Hull-House activity was centered around clubs such as the Boys' Club, Girls' Club, Plato Club, Dante Club, Woman's Club, Eight-Hour Club, Jane Club, and the Working People's Social Science Club. The Social Science Club, particularly, was responsible for Hull-House's early reputation as a haven for radicalism, for it sponsored an open and free discussion forum where there was no censoring of ideas.

Jane Addams encouraged such free-spirited discussion. She was a defender of civil liberties even before there was any organized movement to protect them. Like her friend Clarence Darrow, she insisted that all minorities must have the right to speak, no matter how unpopular their views. Despite violent press opposition and misrepresentation, she remained firm in her belief that even the "despised" must be permitted free speech and press. Such sentiments were dangerous, particularly in Chicago at that time as the city still had not recovered from the tumult of the Haymarket bomb (see Altgeld, pp. 121 ff.).

This did not deter Hull-House from acting as a host to many visitors, including musicians, authors, statesmen and intellectuals from the United States and abroad. At the turn of the century, Peter Kropotkin, the Russian prince who had renounced his title to join the ranks of the Russian revolutionaries, was a guest at Hull-House. Kropotkin was entertained not only by the radicals but also by some of the city's most respectable citizens, including leaders of Chicago society. His visit at Hull-House attracted little attention until two years later, when President William McKinley was assassinated. Kropotkin's stay at the settlement house then became the basis of attacks against it when McKinley's assassin confessed that he had been influenced by anarchist teachings. The police believed there was a widespread plot in the assassination and arrested anyone suspected of being an anarchist.

Abraham Isaak, editor of an anarchist paper, was one of those arrested after the President's murder. Isaak's home was ransacked as the police searched for incriminating literature. In jail the editor was kept incommunicado, not even allowed to see a lawyer. Jane Addams had met the editor once during Kropotkin's stay at Hull-House. He impressed her as an idealist who questioned the social order with a libertarian philosophy. Therefore, when a group of Isaak's friends came to Miss Addams asking for help, she promised the delegation that she would see to it that his rights were protected.

With a friend she went to the mayor and was allowed to visit the prisoner; eventually she received permission for him to see a lawyer. Finally, Abraham Isaak was released, innocent of any implication in the assassination.

Miss Addams regarded her visit to the anarchist editor in prison as no different from a visit to any unfortunate who had been put into jail. This time, however, upon her return to Hull-House, she was greeted by reporters. She had become guilty by association for defending an unpopular political dissenter. "I at once discovered that whether or not I had helped a brother out of a pit, I had fallen into a deep one myself," she reflected.

There were letters of congratulations for her action, too, including one from a federal judge she did not know, and one from a professor in constitutional law who commended her for not giving way to panic but remaining true to her ideals.

A major supporter of Hull-House, a wealthy society lady of national reputation, however, withdrew her help to the settlement house. Miss Addams commented, as she did many times before and afterward in similar circumstances, "We do what we have to do, and if we lose one group of friends by certain actions we'll gain others."

In 1912, though women's suffrage was still a goal to be obtained and Jane Addams could not vote in the Presidential election, Theodore Roosevelt, who had split with the Republican party, sought her support in his candidacy for President on the Progressive party ticket. He had long admired her and considered her "the most useful citizen in Chicago." She, in turn, liked the social justice platform of his party, its demand for women's suffrage, direct primaries, various industrial reforms, and its call for the initiative and referendum which would allow the voter to initiate laws outside of the legislature and to vote on them. She became a member of the platform committee and seconded the nomination of Theodore Roosevelt at the Progressive party convention. She campaigned through eight states for him. The newspapers credited Miss Addams with getting a million votes for her candidate, and though Roosevelt, the Progressive, beat Republican William Howard Taft, both lost to the Democratic candidate, Woodrow Wilson.

From the Presidential campaign, Miss Addams's activity turned almost immediately to the world situation. Europe was moving toward war. The social worker and reformer had been a pacifist for a long time. Perhaps her first stand against militarism was in 1896 when she found a group of boys around Hull-House playing with wooden guns and she suggested that they get long-handled shovels instead—to clean the streets in the ward.

In January 1915 she was elected chairman of the newly formed Women's Peace Party which called for a congress of neutral nations to seek peace in Europe. Three months later, in The Hague, Jane Addams chaired the International Congress of Women at which delegates from twelve nations adopted a resolution demanding a conference of neutral nations to sit in continuous mediation.

Dr. Aletta Jacobs of Holland, one of the conveners of the congress, reminded delegates from such nations as England, Germany, Austria, Italy, Poland, Belgium, United States, Denmark, Norway, and Sweden that "those of us who have convened this Congress . . . have never called it a peace Congress but an International Congress of Women assembled to protest against war, and to suggest steps which may lead to warfare becoming an impossibility."

The Congress of Women, including representatives from belligerent and neutral nations, named a delegation to visit European statesmen to obtain their reactions to the continuous mediation proposal. Jane Addams and Dr. Jacobs were named to one of the delegations. Meeting with prime ministers, presidents, and foreign ministers in London, Berlin, Vienna, Budapest, Rome, Berne, Paris, Le Havre, the ladies stressed that there must be a beginning of negotiation "unless the war continue year after year and at last be terminated through sheer exhaustion."

Practically all of the statesmen were ready to stop the war immediately if only an honorable peace could be provided; some admitted they liked the continuous mediation plan. Miss Addams and Dr. Jacobs met with Prime Minister Stürgkh of Austria and briefed him on their errand. "It may seem very foolish," said Jane Addams, "that women go about in this way; but, after all, the world itself is so strange in this war situation that our mission may be no more strange or foolish than the rest."

"Foolish?" the minister shouted. "Not at all. These are the first sensible words that have been uttered in this room for ten months. That door opens from time to time, and people come in to say, 'Mr. Minister, we must have more men, we must have more ammunition, we must have more money or we cannot go on with this war.' At last the door opens and two people walk in and say, 'Mr. Minister, why not substitute negotiations for fighting?' They are the sensible ones." He banged his fist on his desk for emphasis. "Why not substitute negotiations for fighting," he repeated as he expressed deep interest in their mission.

Jane Addams, returning to the United States in July 1915, exuberantly reported at a Carnegie Hall, New York, meeting that the foreign offices with whom the delegation had met agreed with the women's mission, and these foreign offices favored "a continuous convention of neutrals" which might lead the warring nations to peace. She felt the American public also approved of this sentiment. Immediately after the meeting she left for Washington, D. C., for an interview with President Woodrow Wilson, who would not commit himself on the proposal.

In the meantime, Henry Ford, founder of the Ford Motor Company, volunteered to finance a neutral conference in Europe. He chartered a "peace ship" (*Oskar II*) to carry a delegation of private citizens to Europe as a commission for continuous mediation. A grandiose idea, it became melodramatic when Ford announced he would have the boys out of the trenches by Christmas, less than a month away.

Jane Addams had agreed to sail with the Ford peace ship though she "felt distrust of the publicity involved in the charter of a special vessel." Three days before the departure date, however, she was hospitalized with pleuropneumonia, and the ship sailed without her. Shortly after the ship reached Europe, the project was dissipated.

While Miss Addams was recuperating, both President Wilson and his Republican rival, Charles Evans Hughes, tried to win her endorsement in the 1916 Presidential election. In mid-October she announced that she would cast her first Presidential vote for Woodrow Wilson. She was too ill to enter the campaign actively and all she could do was to vote for him. (In 1913, women could vote in twelve states, including Illinois; nationwide suffrage was granted to women with the nineteenth amendment in 1920.)

Despite Wilson's "he-kept-us-out-of-war" campaign,

events in Europe moved the United States toward war, and as the country began seriously to prepare for it, Jane Addams protested and agitated against the conscription of American men.

When war was declared she defended the rights of conscientious objectors. She was among the earliest supporters of the American Union Against Militarism, the first organized civil liberties movement, out of which grew the American Civil Liberties Union. Jane Addams was one of the ACLU founders and a member of its national committee for a decade. Two months after Congress declared war, she spoke at the Congregational Church in Evanston, Illinois, on "Pacifism and Patriotism—Time of War." She observed then, "The pacifist is making a venture into a new international ethics. . . . The pacifist must serve his country by forcing definitions if possible."

In the audience was Illinois Supreme Court Justice Orrin Carter. He signaled the chairman that he had some comments.

"I have been a lifelong friend of Miss Addams," he began. "I have agreed with her on most questions in the past."

"That sounds as if you are going to break with me," said Miss Addams, laughing.

"I am going to break with you because I think that anything that may tend to cast doubt on the justice of our cause in the present war is very unfortunate. In my opinion, no pacifist measures should be taken until the war is over."

This short exchange between the judge and Miss Addams was headlined in the nation's newspapers. But war or no war, Jane Addams insisted, her views on "the invalidity of war as a method of settlement of social problems" remained unalterable.

Hers was one of the lonely voices. The residents at Hull-House generally did not agree with her pacifist views. Most supported the war. Her fellow social workers did not endorse her stand either. The president of the National Federation of Settlements released a statement to the press, saying, "It has been very painful to many of us who hold Miss Addams in deep affection and wholly respect her, to find that we cannot think or act in unison with her."

Despite her pacifism, during the war years Jane Addams worked with Herbert Hoover, who headed the Food Administration, in urging food conservation as the only way the civilian populations in much of the world could survive.

After the Armistice, the Hull-House lady continued to devote her talents and activity to world peace. She urged entry of the United States into the League of Nations; she called for disarmament; she presided at various conferences of the Women's International League for Peace and Freedom, an organization of which she was a founder. At the 1919 convention in Zurich, she observed, "We shall have to learn to use moral energy, to put a new sort of force into the world *and believe that it is a vital thing*—the only thing, in this moment of sorrow and death and destruction, that will heal the world."

In the era of the "red raids" after World War I, conducted by the United States Attorney General A. Mitchell Palmer, when a dissenting opinion made one a Communist suspect, Jane Addams became a target for the extreme fringe of "100 percent super-patriots" because of her defense of political minorities. Her name appeared on a Senate committee blacklist as certain patriotic organizations labeled her a "dangerous citizen." During the furor, however, Newton D. Baker, United States Secretary of War, observed that Jane Addams "lends dignity and greatness to any list in which her name appears."

After more than ten years of unpopularity and criticisms, the honors began to come again to Miss Addams. Her efforts for world peace were recognized when, in 1931, she was co-winner with Dr. Nicholas Murray Butler of the Nobel Peace Prize. Sickness, however, prevented her from participating in the international event. The day she was to receive the award, she was recuperating in a Baltimore hospital from major surgery—the removal of a tumor. The American minister at Oslo accepted the Gold Peace Medal for her. Professor Halvan Koht of the Nobel Prize Committee spoke about both Dr. Butler and Miss Addams but devoted most of his remarks to the social worker. "She is the foremost woman of her nation, not far from being its greatest citizen," he said. Her hospital room overflowed with flowers, telegrams, and letters—from President Hoover and United States General of the Armies John J. Pershing as well as from friends and clubs at Hull-House.

Miss Addams gave the $16,000 Nobel prize money to the Women's International League. "For years," she explained, "I've been asking people for money for peace, and so it seemed a little inconsistent when I got a little money of my own not to give it to the cause for peace." Earlier, she had been awarded $10,000 for humanitarian achievement. This money she turned over to the social welfare movement in Chicago.

During the 1932 Presidential election, in the midst of a depression, she endorsed Republican Herbert Hoover for reelection. Soon thereafter, however, she praised the new President, Franklin Delano Roosevelt, stressing that no one is "doing more in the direction of sane readjustment at the present moment than the President . . . and the group about him."

When the Women's International League celebrated its twentieth anniversary on May 2, 1935, with a dinner in Washington, D. C., it honored its founder and honorary chairman, Miss Jane Addams. The ballroom was crowded with more than a thousand people —government officials, social settlement workers, writers, lawyers, labor union representatives—all friends and admirers of Jane Addams. Among the speakers at the dinner were Mrs. Eleanor Roosevelt, wife of the President of the United States, Sidney Hillman, president of the Amalgamated Clothing Workers of America, who remembered Jane Addams from the early days of the union's organization and its 1910 strike in Chicago, and Secretary of the Interior Harold Ickes who as a young lawyer in Chicago aided her in the defense of several of her "boys." They all paid homage to her for her never-ending fight for justice and a better social order, for her leadership and crusading spirit.

Then Miss Addams was introduced. Her voice was clear and firm. Sometimes fingering her necklace of beads, sometimes clasping her hands behind her back, she confessed to a hope of modifying human behavior. She suggested that perhaps it was too soon after the war to speak of internationalism but that the day would come when men would be willing to act together. She urged that when that time came the world should be ready with the League of Nations, with the World Court, and with a knowledgeable public opinion. She charged that a lack of moral enterprise was the source of the world's problems.

"At least we can seek to remove the difficulties which arise from each nation seeking to get the most for itself," she continued. "It would be a splendid thing if the United States could lead the world in a new type of international relationship. . . . We move slowly, and yet much has occurred in twenty years." She stressed that the world was still suffering from war psychology. Public opinion must decide that war is futile and killing is never justified.

"We may be a long way from permanent peace," she concluded. "We need education of ourselves; of others; development of public opinion; moral enterprise."

She returned to Chicago, resuming work on a biography of Julia Lathrop, meeting with Hull-House residents to tell them about her Washington experiences. On May 15, 1935, she began to complain of a severe pain in her left side, and two days later her physician ordered her to the hospital. He had found signs of an acute infection but could not make a definite diagnosis. The next day she underwent abdominal surgery. On May 21, 1935, she died from the advanced cancer the doctors had found during the surgery.

The delicate, sensitive Cedarville child who had felt a responsibility to save the world at age seven was dead at seventy-four, acclaimed one of the great citizens of the world. Her body lay at rest in Hull-House where all day and night a thousand persons an hour passed before the casket. Businessmen and professionals whose lives had been influenced by Hull-House and younger men who were now members of the settlement stood as an honor guard. A simple funeral service was held in the central court of Hull-House, and the body was taken to Cedarville, Illinois, where she was buried in the family plot.

The Illinois State Senate lauded her as "one of the foremost citizens of Illinois," but an immigrant workman of the Hull-House neighborhood summed up this woman who had devoted her life to all of humanity by saying, "She not just one people, her not just one religion. Her all people, all religions."

Jane Addams's dream for peace with justice remains unfulfilled in a world still torn by war. Her monument as a social worker stands with Hull-

House, today an association of seven settlements scattered in various needy neighborhoods of Chicago. One is named the Jane Addams Center. Another affiliate with the Hull-House complex is named in honor of her friend Clarence Darrow. Only the original Hull-House building remains on Halsted Street. It houses some of Jane Addams's papers and awards and is part of the University of Illinois Chicago Circle campus. Hull-House today is a "little house" on the university's new campus in the midst of large, starkly modern buildings. The surrounding neighborhood is still a ghetto of the poor.

Robert Green Ingersoll

ROBERT GREEN INGERSOLL
1833-1899
Agnostic and Republican

THE FATHER was a "hellfire and brimstone" preacher, an evangelist who preached a dogma of eternal damnation and torment. The son, Robert Green Ingersoll, was among the world's great freethinkers who questioned the existence of hell and encouraged man to look for heaven on earth. He was accused of corrupting souls by his anti-religious teachings, and mothers frightened their children by threatening that "Pagan Bob" would get them if they did not behave. Yet Ingersoll lived his life according to the ethical and philanthropic Christian principle of love. A gentle man who believed in the sanctity of the home, he extended his boundless affection to all of humanity.

"Whosoever crossed the threshold of his home," commented a friend, "entered paradise." His youngest daughter once whimsically observed of him, "My father was not a man. He was a god!"

Ingersoll gave up a political career which could have led to the White House and, instead, used his oratorical skills to preach a religion based on humanism: "Human intelligence, applied to human conduct, is what we call morality; and you add to simple morality kindness, charity, love—and there can be no more perfect religion imagined by the brain of man."

With his name almost forgotten except for an occasional brief mention in history books or at freethinker conclaves, it is difficult to imagine his popularity on the lecture platform during the last three decades of the nineteenth century. Tens of thousands heard him lecture then and applauded as he lashed out at superstition, myth, and orthodox religion, as he praised Thomas Paine and Voltaire and interpreted Shakespeare and Robert Burns. And it is perhaps equally difficult to imagine—today, when religious fundamentalism has lost its impact as a relevant issue—how heartily he was despised by those whom his ideas offended. He called himself an agnostic, which he defined as an individual who "says he does not know—that he knows nothing about the supernatural—nothing as to origin—nothing as to destiny—and consequently does not pretend to know and willingly waits."

Robert Green Ingersoll was born in Dresden, New York, on August 11, 1833. His father, John Ingersoll—sometimes referred to as "Priest" Ingersoll—was forced to shift from one church to another because of his courageous but unpopular stand against Negro slavery. Priest Ingersoll's sermons for abolition were as fearless and as forceful as his exhortations to sinners to save their souls. Although most congregations approved his "hell and brimstone" approach to religion, they did not appreciate his views on chattel slavery; and so the family moved, from New York to Ohio, to Wisconsin, to Michigan, to Indiana, to Kentucky, and, finally, to Illinois.

The Ingersoll genealogy can be traced to pre-Revolutionary days in America. John Ingersoll's father had been a soldier with the American Revolutionary forces at Bunker Hill. The preacher himself married Mary Livingston, reportedly a collateral descendant of Chancellor Robert R. Livingston who administered the oath of office of President of the United States to George Washington. She was also an abolitionist and among the first women to prepare and sign a petition calling for the abolition of slavery in Washington, D. C. She had read Thomas Paine's *The Age of Reason* and had reservations about orthodox religion. Nevertheless, she was a good wife to the Reverend John Ingersoll, helping him as he tended to the spiritual needs of his congregation.

Of their five children—two daughters and three sons—the eldest son, John, Jr., and both daughters shared their father's religious attitudes. The two youngest boys, Robert and Ebon Clark, were freethinkers, questioners of orthodox religion.

Mary Ingersoll died at the age of thirty-six, when Robert was only two years old. In the years following, the Reverend Mr. Ingersoll married twice more; yet between father and children the relationship remained close and affectionate.

A revivalist with a penchant for long sermons, Priest Ingersoll started preaching on the Sabbath morning and ended at sundown. Robert Ingersoll reminisced about these Sundays in his lecture "The Liberty of Man, Woman and Child." When he was a boy, he said, Sunday was considered "altogether too holy to be happy in. When the sun fell below the horizon on Saturday evening, there was a darkness fell upon the house ten thousand times deeper than that of night. Nobody said a pleasant word; nobody laughed; nobody smiled; the child that looked the sickest was regarded as the most pious. . . . If you were caught chewing gum it was only another evidence of the total depravity of the human heart."

On Saturday night everybody "looked sad and mournful. . . . On Sunday morning the solemnity had simply increased. Then we went to church. The minister was in a pulpit about twenty feet high, with a little sounding-board above him, and he commenced at 'firstly' and went on and on and on to about 'twenty-thirdly' . . . and then took a general view of the subject, and in about two hours reached the last chapter in Revelation."

Following intermission, there was catechism. Then "the minister asked us if we knew that we all deserved to go to hell, and we all answered 'Yes.' Then we were asked if we would be willing to go to hell if it was God's will, and every little liar shouted 'Yes.'

"Then the same sermon was preached once more, commencing at the other end and going back."

The procession home from church was always sad and solemn. If the weather was warm and if the children had been obedient, they would be taken out to the graveyard "to cheer us up a little. It did cheer me," Ingersoll sardonically recalled. "When I looked at the sunken tombs and the leaning stones, and read the half-effaced inscriptions through the moss of silence and forgetfulness, it was a great comfort. The reflection came to my mind that the observance of the Sabbath could not last always."

Sunday finally passed, and "when the last rim of light sank below the horizon, off would go our caps, and we would give three cheers for liberty once more."

There was never a time in Ingersoll's life when he did not question theological tenets. He once commented in amusement that the first thing he found in the Bible was a "contradiction." One Bible had the date of his birth as August 12, 1833; in a second family Bible he found the entry of his birth as August 11, 1833. "I have continued to find contradictions in the Sacred Volume all my life."

As a young boy he had listened to hundreds of sermons, but the most vivid in his memory and one he felt was a turning point in his religious thinking was delivered by a Baptist minister who painted such a dreadful picture of hell and eternal punishment that Robert's mind was set in revolt against orthodox and fundamentalist religion. "Your religion is a lie," he shouted.

Some of his antagonists charged that Robert Ingersoll questioned his father's religion—and all traditional religion—because of his father's unkind treatment of him as a boy. Ingersoll denied this. Time and time again he answered that charge, always insisting, "This is an orthodox lie. The bigots, unable to meet my arguments, are endeavoring to dig open the grave and calumniate the dead. My father was one of the most affectionate of men, and in his treatment of his children was kindness itself." Many times the son stressed, "My father was infinitely better than the religion he preached."

The theological differences between father and son seem never to have marred their love for each other. As the years passed, Priest Ingersoll's theology became less dogmatic, and to such an extent that on his death bed he asked his agnostic son to read to him Plato's "Death of Socrates."

Robert's early education was informal and meager. Much of it consisted of memorizing Greek, Hebrew, and Latin passages which his father, a scholar of languages, prescribed as he took charge of the initial stages of his sons' education. Robert's formal training was a short period in grammar school, then in a private school which met in the basement of his father's church. From the reading of the Bible in his father's household, he turned to the works of Cowper, Byron, and Shelley, Paine and Voltaire, Socrates and Epicurus, Comte, Petrarch, Burns, and Shakespeare.

In 1852, at the age of nineteen, he became a teacher in a "subscription school" in Illinois, where the young teacher's compensation came partially from room and board with the families of his students. He was popular with the students, who enjoyed his humor and his ability to make study interesting.

A group of revivalists had a room-and-board arrangement at the same house where Ingersoll was staying. They devoted much of their dinner table conversation to religion. The young teacher refrained from participating, but one evening the revivalists, knowing of his religious doubts, insisted on hearing his views on baptism, and taunted him for his answer. Ingersoll snapped, "Baptism is a good thing, a very good thing . . . with soap."

The revivalists were aghast, and members of the community, hearing of this remark, were horrified. Baptism to many of them was a meaningful rite and was never to be discussed so flippantly. If such witticism was an indication of what the teacher really believed, the school board felt, he could no longer be trusted to teach the community's children. They dismissed him.

Ingersoll then began to study law in a lawyer's office. His brother Ebon was already preparing for his law career, and this inspired Robert to do the same. Both brothers were admitted to the bar in Mount Vernon, Illinois, on December 20, 1854, Robert at the age of twenty-one, Ebon at twenty-three.

E. C. Ingersoll and R. G. Ingersoll hung up their first shingle—"Attorneys and Counsellors at Law"—in Shawneetown, Illinois. Their partnership continued until Ebon's death in 1879, although it was interrupted for a while when the older brother was elected in 1856 to a two-year term in the Illinois state legislature. During this period, Robert Ingersoll rode the circuit from one courthouse to another, traveling by horse and buggy or on horseback through scores of counties as he represented clients in criminal and civil cases.

While living in Shawneetown, Robert Ingersoll delivered his first public address. A local minister who was scheduled to speak at a town picnic was unable to come. A member of the planning committee asked Ingersoll to say "a few words of devotional importance."

Ingersoll had just finished reading Thomas Paine. He was impressed with the American revolutionary's deism and his skepticism about religion, and he was angry with Paine's critics. After a few words of "devotional importance," the young lawyer spent the rest of the time lauding his new hero. The farmers, who formed a large part of the community, liked Ingersoll's oratory, his agility with words, his eloquence. The planning committee members, however, were resentful. They were bitter that Ingersoll had used the occasion to eulogize Paine. Most of them probably would have agreed with President Theodore Roosevelt's denunciation of Paine more than a half-century later when he called this American revolutionary a "dirty little atheist," although Paine was neither "dirty" nor an "atheist." Ingersoll's remarks at the picnic on Thomas Paine were eventually expanded into a full lecture in which he praised Paine as doing more than any man to convince the people of America—at a time when they merely shouted "taxation without representation is tyranny"—that they "ought to separate from Great Britain" and "ought to found a representative government."

At the close of the American Revolution, Ingersoll asserted, "no man stood higher in America" than Paine, but this was before he published his *Age of Reason*. With its publication, Paine became despised, shunned. Much of Ingersoll's reported affinity to Paine is based on this book. Both Ingersoll and Paine denied the inspiration of the Scriptures, believing that true religion meant doing justice, showing mercy, endeavoring to make others happy; both had a sensitive religious—if heretical—spirit.

When Ebon Ingersoll's term as Illinois state representative expired, the brothers moved to Peoria. They wanted a bigger town, wider horizons, and Peoria offered this. Here, too, the Ingersoll brothers entered politics. The Stephen Douglas Democrats in 1860, seeking a nominee for the United States Congress from the Peoria district, looked to the Ingersoll brothers. Ebon Ingersoll suggested that Robert be the candidate, and the decision was unanimous.

Immediately, Robert Ingersoll challenged his Republican opponent, Judge William B. Kellogg, who was seeking reelection, to a series of debates, similar to those of Lincoln and Douglas two years earlier. The issues were almost identical: the Republicans opposed the extension of slavery into the territories and wanted

Congress to enact such a law, while the Douglas Democrats believed the territories themselves should decide whether or not to permit slavery.

Furthermore, Judge Kellogg defended the Fugitive Slave law, while Ingersoll shocked both Republicans and Douglas Democrats when he declared: "The Fugitive Slave law is the most infamous enactment that ever disgraced a statute book." To Ingersoll, the law urged citizens to aid and abet a crime—the crime of slavery: "The man who approves or apologizes for that infamy is a brute!" Though he did not win the election, the debates gave him the opportunity to display his oratorical artistry and his resonant voice, and helped to establish his reputation as an effective public speaker.

In 1862 a farmer retained Ingersoll to defend him against a murder charge. The young attorney, believing his client could not get a fair trial in Peoria, asked for a change of venue. When this was granted, the trial was moved to Groveland, a few miles from Peoria.

In Groveland lived the Benjamin Weld Parker family, nonbelievers, admirers of Paine and Voltaire, and of Ingersoll, whom they had once heard lecture. During the murder trial, the Parkers invited Ingersoll to their home for dinner, where he met their daughter Eva and fell in love with her. They were married on February 13, 1862, after a brief courtship.

The Civil War was already raging. Ingersoll, who had been active in initiating defense mobilization for the

Union, was commissioned a colonel of one of the three regiments he had raised. Within weeks after his marriage, the regiment was mustered into the army. In December 1862 Ingersoll led his cavalry into battle at Lexington, Tennessee, but they were outnumbered in men and weapons. The regiment fled. Ingersoll, however, taken prisoner by the Confederate army, was released on parole. Eventually he resigned his commission, and on June 30, 1863, was honorably discharged from the Union army.

Ingersoll returned to Peoria and resumed his successful law practice. When he had entered the military, he had been a Douglas Democrat, unhappy with Abraham Lincoln's Inaugural Address in which the President-elect upheld the validity of the Fugitive Slave law. Ingersoll emerged from the war a Republican, an admirer of Lincoln primarily because of Lincoln's Emancipation Proclamation. Eulogizing the President after his death, he observed that Lincoln "neither knelt nor scorned. With him, men were neither great nor small—they were right or wrong. Nothing discloses real character like the use of power. It is easy for the weak to be gentle. Most people can bear adversity. But if you wish to know what a man really is, give him power. This is the supreme test. It is the glory of Lincoln that, having almost absolute power, he never abused it, except on the side of mercy."

The Colonel became active in Republican politics, and in early 1867 was appointed attorney general of Illinois by Governor Richard I. Oglesby. Friends urged him to seek the nomination for governor of Illinois. He wanted the nomination but felt he could not defeat the other contender, General John M. Palmer, though he believed he could be victorious over the Democratic opponent in the statewide election. Only after General Palmer assured his own supporters and Ingersoll that he was not interested in the nomination did Ingersoll resign as attorney general and permit his name to be presented to the convention. At the last moment, however, Palmer changed his mind and became the Republican nominee.

Ingersoll's friends were bitter; he felt betrayed. Disillusioned, he withdrew from any future attempt for elective office.

The next several years were a political hiatus for Robert Ingersoll. But in 1876 he emerged as a national figure with his nominating speech for James G. Blaine of Maine as the Republican party candidate for President. There was some surprise among the delegates when it became known that Robert Ingersoll would make the nomination.

"Isn't his name Ebon Clark Ingersoll?" asked a delegate.

"It must be Ebon, he was the congressman from Illinois," said another.

A delegate from Illinois answered, "His name is Robert. He's Ebon's brother. He's Illinois's greatest orator, and when he gets through with his nominating speech today he will be known as the nation's greatest orator."

The delegate's prediction came true. Ingersoll's elaborate oratory—he referred to his candidate as "an armed warrior," "a plumed knight"—was received with extraordinary enthusiasm by the delegates at the convention and the nation's newspapers. Although Blaine failed to get the nomination, Ingersoll scored a personal success for his "impassioned, artful, brilliant, and persuasive" speech; he was reported to have "swept the whole body like a tumultuous flood." A later historian, with twentieth-century skepticism, termed this address as a "stupendous galimatias," but in Ingersoll's time flowery political bombast was in style. He was subsequently flooded with demands for lecture engagements.

During the Presidential campaign that followed, Ingersoll spoke at Chicago's Exposition Building to one of the largest audiences ever assembled under one roof to hear a single speaker. "I am proud that I belong to the Republican party," he told the audience. "It is the only party that has said: 'There shall be no distinction on account of race, on account of color, on account of previous condition [of servitude]!'

"In my judgment, the black people have suffered enough. . . . And allow me to say again to impress it forever upon every man that hears me, you will always be the inferior of the man you wrong. Every race is inferior to the race it tramples upon and robs."

Frederick Douglass, the Negro journalist, orator, and antislavery leader, recalled in his autobiography the time he mentioned to a friend that he was going to Peoria, Illinois. Douglass dreaded this visit because the last time he had been in that city no room was available in any hotel for a black man. He feared he might meet "a similar exclusion" on this trip.

His friend told Douglass, "I know a man in Peoria and if you cannot get a hotel room there, he would gladly open his doors to you. He is a man who will receive you at any hour of the night, and in any weather. His name is Robert Ingersoll . . . he will be glad to welcome you at midnight or at cock-crow." Although Douglass did get a hotel room this time, he was so impressed with the description of Ingersoll he determined to meet him. Douglass wrote of that meeting, "If I have ever met a man with real living human sunshine in his face and honest, manly kindness in his voice, I met one who possessed these qualities. I received a welcome from Mr. Ingersoll and his family which would have been a cordial to the bruised heart of any proscribed and storm-beaten stranger and one which I can never forget or fail to appreciate."

During the 1876 political tour, Ingersoll spoke before the Veteran Soldiers of the Rebellion. This address to the Civil War veterans contains one of his most famous and widely quoted oratorical passages, the "Vision of War." While these lines may seem trite today, when Ingersoll read his prepared speeches they aroused his audience to high emotion.

"The past rises before me like a dream. Again we are in the great struggle for national life. We hear the sounds of preparation—the music of boisterous drums—the silver voices of heroic bugles. We see thousands of assemblages, and hear the appeals of orators. We see the pale cheeks of women, and the flushed faces of men; and in those assemblages we see all the dead whose dust we have covered with flowers. . . .

"I have one sentiment for soldiers living and dead: cheers for the living; tears for the dead."

Despite this patriotic oratory, Ingersoll tended to antimilitarism, as indicated in one of his famous orations, "A Soliloquy at the Tomb of Napoleon":

"A little while ago, I stood by the grave of the old Napoleon. . . . I thought of the orphans and widows he had made, of the tears that had been shed for his glory, and of the only woman who ever loved him, pushed from his heart by the cold hand of ambition. And I said I would rather have been a French peasant and worn wooden shoes. I would rather have lived in a hut with a vine growing over the door, and the grapes growing purple in the kisses of the autumn sun. I would rather have been that poor peasant with my loving wife by my side, knitting as the day died out of the sky—with my children upon my knees and their arms about me—I would rather have been that man and gone down to the tongueless silence of the dreamless dust, than to have been that imperial impersonation of force and murder, known as 'Napoleon the Great.' "

Ingersoll always spoke in grandiose terms. He was magniloquent in his political oratory as well as on the freethought lecture platform. He was also politically obtuse. It was not unusual for the Republican Ingersoll to charge: "Every man that tries to destroy the nation is a Democrat," or "I belong to the party that believes in good crops . . . the Democratic party is a party of famines." As Clarence Darrow observed years later, Ingersoll clung to old political superstitions with a peculiar blindness. Darrow suggested that "99 out of every 100 who agreed with him on the religious question differed from him on political matters." Ingersoll's greatest speeches were nonpolitical: his eulogy to his brother Ebon, who died in 1879, which is a classic among tributes to the dead; and his courtroom and lecture hall expressions of humanism, agnosticism, and the right to personal freedom and dignity.

Ingersoll neither affirmed nor denied the existence of God; he said he did not know, that no one knows whether God exists. Based on this premise, he evolved his philosophy of religion. The lecture which made him famous as a freethinker was "The Gods," initially delivered in 1871. In it he paraphrased Alexander Pope: "An honest God is the boldest work of Man," and pointed out that "each nation has created a god, and the god has always resembled his creators. He hated and loved what they hated and loved, and he was invariably found on the side of those in power."

Infidels have struggled for the rights of man all through the ages, Ingersoll said, yet "we are constantly charged by the church with tearing down without building again."

"If you find so much fault with God's work," a

clergyman once challenged him, "will you tell me one single thing that you, if you had the power, would do differently?"

Unhesitantly, Ingersoll smilingly responded: "Why, yes, instead of disease, I'd make good health catching."

His lecture called "Orthodoxy" contained one of Ingersoll's most devastating indictments of orthodox religion. "Religion and science are enemies," he declared. Orthodoxy is a superstition resting on fear and faith. Science, on the other hand, is reason and investigation. "This century will be called Darwin's century. He was one of the greatest men who ever touched this globe. He has explained more of the phenomenon of life than all of the religious teachers." Charles Darwin, the father of the theory of evolution, epitomized science to Ingersoll, who would be known as the "bulldog" of Darwin.

There was no compromise in the popular lecturer's attack on dogmatic religion. He was not a scholar in the academic sense. He was, however, well read in theology, literature, and politics. While Thomas Huxley, who coined the word "agnostic," and other academicians, such as Herbert Spencer and William Graham Sumner, lectured at universities, Ingersoll popularized agnosticism to the world outside.

Ingersoll, in his lecture "Some Mistakes of Moses," concluded that "we cannot please God by believing the improbable; that credulity is not a virtue; that investigation is not a crime; that every mind should be free . . ."

As a nineteenth-century humanist, praising the dignity and worthiness of man and his capacity for self-realization, Ingersoll directed his attacks primarily against the literal interpretation of the Bible which was prevalent among most American religionists of that day. A Methodist minister admitted that "it may be that we have claimed too much for the Bible, and thereby given not a little occasion for such men as Mr. Ingersoll to appear at the other extreme . . ."

While Ingersoll was attracting attention as a great orator, he was at the same time making national newspaper headlines as an attorney. For two years, 1882 and 1883, he was the defense attorney in the "Star Route" case. Star Routes were private companies contracted by the government to haul mail to territories which had no railroad or steamboat connections. The name was derived from the asterisks used by postal registers to designate the routes. Stephen W. Dorsey, a former United States senator from Arkansas and also a former secretary of the Republican National Convention, his brother who was an assistant postmaster general, and four others were indicted for conspiracy and fraud against the United States government in connection with exorbitant rate rises in Star Route contracts. Ingersoll's defense of the Dorsey brothers resulted in a hung jury on the first trial and acquittal in the second.

In the fall of 1886, Ingersoll was invited to join Captain William P. Black as counsel appealing the death sentence of the Haymarket anarchists, the men convicted of throwing the bomb into police ranks during the Haymarket meeting in Chicago (see Altgeld, pp. 121 ff.). Ingersoll declined with the rationale that he believed his becoming associated with the appeal would only further prejudice the case. "The tocsin has already been sounded by the press and pulpit," he declared, "that anarchism is the logical fruit of Ingersollism." He suggested that the defense should look for a lawyer of national prominence who is "a pillar of the church and can cover the men with his conservative life and character."

Though he did not become associated with the defense, Ingersoll did plead with the governor for clemency and a commutation of the sentence. Ingersoll warned that if the men were executed a monument would be erected over their graves and "those who were executed as criminals will be regarded by thousands as saints."

The Haymarket anarchists were buried in Waldheim cemetery near Chicago. Over their graves was erected a massive sculptured monument. Each November 11, on the anniversary of the execution, a group of men, women, and children visit the cemetery, pay homage to "our martyrs," and place a wreath at the foot of the monument.

In May 1887 Robert Ingersoll defended Charles B. Reynolds on the charge of blasphemy. Reynolds faced a fine of two hundred dollars or twelve months imprisonment or both if convicted. Ingersoll told a jury in the Circuit Court in Morristown, New Jersey: "I regard this as one of the most important cases that can be submitted to a jury. It is not a case that involves a little property, neither is it one that involves simply the liberty of one man. It involves the freedom of speech, the intellectual liberty of every citizen of New Jersey."

Reynolds, a preacher turned atheist, came to the town of Boonton, New Jersey, adjacent to Morristown, in the summer of 1886, secured some land, pitched a tent, and announced "free-thought" meetings. The churches of Boonton objected; some of the townspeople invaded the tent, hurled rotten eggs at Reynolds; some slashed the canvas and cut the ropes of the tent.

That fall Reynolds distributed his free-thought pamphlets in Morristown. A Boonton delegation confronted him. They and the Morristown religious community clamored for his indictment on the charge of blasphemy. The grand jury returned a two-count indictment—one for blasphemy at Boonton, the second for blasphemy at Morristown. Reynolds furnished the five hundred dollar bond and was released on bail pending the outcome of the trial.

On May 19, 1887, court convened. A jury was selected, and the prosecutor proceeded to call sixteen witnesses who testified that Reynolds had given them the allegedly blasphemous pamphlet. Ingersoll, in his cross-examination, tried unsuccessfully to get the witnesses to admit they had read the pamphlet.

"I do not know that I shall have any witnesses one way or the other," the defense attorney told the court. "Perhaps after dinner, I may feel like making a few remarks."

"There will be great disappointment if you do not," said the judge as he adjourned court for a dinner recess.

When court reconvened, Ingersoll rose, started to speak from the defense table, then walked toward the jury, and remained there for his two-hour plea:

"Gentlemen of the Jury: . . . The question to be tried by you is whether a man has the right to express his honest thought; and for that reason there can be no case of greater importance submitted to a jury. . . . I deny the right of any man, of any number of men, of any church, of any State, to put a padlock on the lips—to make the tongue a convict. I passionately deny the right of the Herod of authority to kill the children of the brain."

Ingersoll paused, looked at the jury of twelve men, asked, "What is blasphemy?

"Nobody knows," he answered his own question, "unless he takes into consideration where he is.

"What is blasphemy in one country would be a religious exhortation in another. It is owing to where you are and who is in authority. . . .

"To enslave your fellowman, to put chains upon his body—that is blasphemy.

"To enslave the minds of men, to put manacles upon the brain, padlocks upon the lips—that is blasphemy.

"To deny what you believe to be true, to admit to be true what you believe to be a lie—that is blasphemy.

"To strike the weak and unprotected, in order that you may gain the applause of the ignorant and superstitious mob—that is blasphemy.

"To persecute the intelligent few, at the command of the ignorant many—that is blasphemy.

"To forge chains, to build dungeons, for your honest fellowmen—that is blasphemy.

"To pollute the souls of children with the dogma of eternal pain—that is blasphemy.

"To violate your conscience—that is blasphemy.

"The jury that gives an unjust verdict, and the judge who pronounces an unjust sentence, are blasphemers.

"The man who bows to public opinion against his better judgment and against his honest conviction, is a blasphemer. . . .

"I presume that each one of you has the good of what you call Christianity at heart. If you have, I beg of you to acquit this man. If you believe Christianity to be a good, it never can do any church any good to put a man in jail for the expression of opinion. Any church that imprisons a man because he has used an argument against its creed, will simply convince the world that it cannot answer the argument."

As he asked for a verdict of not guilty, Ingersoll concluded, "I sincerely hope that it will never be necessary again, under the flag of the United States . . . for a man to stand before a jury and plead for the Liberty of Speech."

The jury in the Reynolds case found the defendant guilty, and the judge imposed a lenient twenty-five dollar fine. As Ingersoll was leaving the courtroom, an old man approached him, extended his hand, and said, "Colonel Ingersoll, I am a Presbyterian pastor, but I must say that was the noblest speech in defense of liberty I ever heard! Your hand, sir; your hand."

The editor of the prestigious *North American Review* invited Ingersoll and the Reverend Dr. Henry M. Field, editor of the *New York Evangelist*, to participate in a literary discussion on Christianity. The articles appeared in late 1887 and early 1888. Dr. Field started the series with "An Open Letter to Robert G. Ingersoll."

"I am glad that I know you," Dr. Field opened, "even though some of my brethren look upon you as a monster because of your unbelief."

Dr. Field found many points of sympathy with the agnostic. He stressed that he, too, had an "intense hatred of superstition" and that Ingersoll "cannot loathe it more than I do. But unfortunately you do not limit your crusade to the religions of Asia, but turn the same style of argument against the religions of Europe and America, and, indeed, against the religious belief and worship of every country and clime.

"You are waging a hopeless war," the famous minister continued, "a war in which you are certain only of defeat. The Christian religion began to be nearly two thousand years before you and I were born, and it will live two thousand years after we are dead. What is it that it lives on and on, while nations and kingdoms perish? Is not this 'survival of the fittest'?"

The contestants had two other exchanges when into the verbal battle came the Honorable William E. Gladstone, member of the British Parliament and an Episcopalian. He wrote, "Whereas the highest self-restraint is necessary in these dark but, therefore, all the more exciting inquiries, in order to maintain the ever quivering balance of our faculties, this rider Ingersoll chooses to ride an unbroken horse, and to throw the reins upon his neck."

Ingersoll replied to Mr. Gladstone by suggesting that "it may be that 'to ride an unbroken horse with the reins thrown upon his neck'—as you charge me with doing—gives a greater variety of sensations, a keener delight, and a better prospect of winning the race than to sit solemnly astride of a dead one, in 'a deep reverential calm,' with the bridle firmly in your hand."

Another participant was a Roman Catholic cardinal, Henry Edward Manning. "The Church is dogmatic for fear of error," he wrote. "Every truth defined adds to its treasure. It narrows the field of error and enlarges the inheritance of truth. The world and the Church are ever moving in opposite directions. As the world becomes more vague and uncertain, the Church becomes more definite."

Ingersoll responded that the Cardinal's case depended upon the intelligence and veracity of his witnesses. "It is very hard, indeed, to prove what the apostles said, or what the fathers of the Church wrote."

Who won the four-way discussion? As with most debates, no one's opinion had been changed. The followers of the religionists claimed victory, as did Ingersoll's admirers, including Thomas Huxley and Walt Whitman.

Ingersoll first met Whitman on the poet's seventieth birthday anniversary in May 1889. He described Whitman as "a sturdy teller of the truth," and said Whitman had "the true American spirit—the spirit destined, as I believe, to become universal." He was "not only the poet of democracy . . . but he was the poet of the human race." Yet there were some passages in *Leaves of Grass* which Ingersoll would have preferred that Whitman had not written. He disliked their eroticism, for Ingersoll was almost prudish, uncompromising in sex ethics, purity, and moral standards as he was in all his attitudes, from Republicanism to agnosticism. Nevertheless, Ingersoll and Whitman respected and admired each other. Whitman saw in Ingersoll "a man whose importance to the time could not be overfigured; not literal importance, not argumentative importance, not antitheological Republican importance, but spiritual importance—importance as a force, as a consuming energy—a fiery blast for the new virtues, which are only old virtues done over for honest use again."

Almost two years later, in March 1891, Ingersoll fulfilled Whitman's wishes that he speak at Whitman's funeral. Ingersoll said on this occasion, "My friends . . . a great man, a great American, the most eminent citizen of this Republic, lies dead before us. . . . He wrote a liturgy for mankind; he wrote a great and splendid psalm of life, and he gave to us the gospel of humanity—the greatest gospel that can be preached."

Ingersoll had originally moved from Peoria to Washington, D. C., after his brother Ebon became a member of Congress in 1864. But Ebon was dead now, and there was little to hold him in the nation's capital. Furthermore, his wife, Eva, longed to move to New York. She argued that during the past winter her husband had spent most of his time in that city both in his law practice and in his Sunday lectures. New York was a mecca of the cultural activities the Ingersolls loved—the theater, concerts, art, books.

They moved there in 1885. Sunday evenings at their home became an event, the guests including businessmen and actors, politicians and freethinkers, writers and statesmen, personalities of the theater and the musical world. Senator Chauncey Depew, industrialist Andrew Carnegie, actress Julia Marlowe, political scientist Henry George, suffragette Elizabeth Cody Stanton, actor Maurice Barrymore, musician Anton Seidl, and writer Elbert Hubbard were all visitors.

For the next four years Ingersoll limited himself to the lecture platform. He delivered his last lecture, "What is Religion?" on June 2, 1899, a little more than a month before he died.

"Real religion," he said, "real worship," is to rouse oneself "to do all useful things, to reach with thought and deed the ideal in your brain, to give your fancies wing, that they, like chemist bees, may find art's nectar in the weeds of common things . . . to increase knowledge, to take burdens from the weak, to develop the brain, to defend the right, to make a palace for the soul. This is real religion. This is real worship."

On July 22, 1899, the Chicago *Tribune* carried a front-page story headlined:

COL. INGERSOLL
DIES SMILING
End Comes Without Warning
to the Noted Agnostic at
His Summer Home at
Dobbs Ferry, N.Y.

His death was attributed to angina pectoris. Ingersoll would have preferred to die slowly, conscious of all that was going on around him. "When I was a young man," he said a few days before his death, "I wanted to die suddenly. No lingering for me. But I have changed now. I want to die slowly. I want to be conscious to the last. I hope to know the sensation of approaching death. I have some things I want to say." But death came suddenly for the famed lecturer. He had been talking with his son-in-law on the porch of his home discussing the previous night's billiard game between them. Ingersoll had succeeded in some difficult shots during that game.

"I'm going upstairs to my room for a moment," he

said to his son-in-law, "and when I come down I can beat you in another game of billiards." The challenge was accepted.

Mrs. Ingersoll went upstairs with her husband. "How do you feel, Papa?" she asked when he seated himself in his favorite chair.

Without replying, he rested his head upon the back of his chair. He smiled, his eyes closed—and the great agnostic was dead at the age of sixty-six.

Funeral services were private, held in Ingersoll's bedroom. There were no speeches, only readings. A friend read Ingersoll's "Declaration of the Free." Another recited from one of his lectures, "The Creed of Science." Robert Ingersoll's tribute to his brother Ebon Clark was also read, and then the body was taken to the cemetery for cremation. The ashes, placed in a bronze urn, remained with Mrs. Ingersoll until her death in 1923. Nine years later the urns of both Mr. and Mrs. Ingersoll were buried in Arlington National Cemetery.

Clarence Darrow, speaking at the memorial meeting for Ingersoll in Chicago shortly after his death, called him "one of the bravest, grandest champions of human liberty the world has ever seen." Mark Twain, who had become friends with Ingersoll when both were speakers at a dinner in November 1879 honoring General Grant, wrote to Ingersoll's niece on the death of his friend, "Except for my daughter's, I have not grieved for any death as I grieved for his." There were other memorials: a bronze statue dedicated to him in Peoria; his birthplace restored; a memorial plaque at

52 Gramercy Park in New York City, site of the Ingersoll home.

Though there always have been voices questioning religious dogma, Robert Ingersoll brought to agnosticism a fervency, a popularity unequaled by anyone else in his time. He was dogmatic in his attack, as dogmatic as the tenets he decried. At a time, however, when religion and the church were primarily interested in the hereafter rather than the now, Ingersoll was among the few who asserted, "We, too, have our religion and it is this: Help for the living. Hope for the dead."

THE CHALLENGE CONTINUES

SOMETIMES their voices were like cries in the wilderness, unheeded, unheard. Yet their words and actions moved a nation to social change as they exposed the evils of their day and proposed roads to freedom and social justice. These dissenters urged personal integrity and understanding among people; they were giants not only in their own areas of endeavor but in the nation as a whole.

Surely party politics is better understood because of Lincoln Steffens.

Labor is stronger because of Eugene Victor Debs.

Freedom of thought and action is safer because of Clarence Darrow.

Men are more politically courageous because of John Peter Altgeld.

The yearning for peace and social well-being is more determined because of Jane Addams.

Organized religion is more resilient and religious beliefs less rigid because of Robert G. Ingersoll.

Every generation has its heroes who are not satisfied with the status quo and look to—and even suffer for—the future. So it was with the dissenters in this book, and so it will be—always.

ACKNOWLEDGMENTS AND SUGGESTED READINGS

WE WANT to express our appreciation to Dr. Carl Hermann Voss who conceived the idea of this book. In his criticisms and suggestions he has been most helpful. Our thanks also to Dr. Stanley L. Chyet of the Hebrew Union College, Cincinnati, for his criticisms and cooperation; and to Newberry Library, Chicago, where we researched this book.

The authors also wish to thank and acknowledge the following authors and publications to whose works reference has been made.

LINCOLN STEFFENS

Darrow, Clarence. *The Story of My Life.* New York, Charles Scribner's Sons, 1934.

Regier, C. C. *The Era of the Muckrakers.* Chapel Hill: University of North Carolina Press, 1932; Gloucester, Mass.: Peter Smith, 1957.

Steffens, Lincoln. *The Autobiography of . . .* (2 vols.) New York: Harcourt, Brace & Co., 1931.

———. *John Reed Under the Kremlin.* Chicago: Walden Book Shop, 1921.

———. *The Letters of . . .* (2 vols.) New York: Harcourt, Brace & Co., 1938.

———. *Moses in Red. The Revolt of Israel as a Typical*

Revolution. Philadelphia: Dorrance & Co., 1926.

———. *The Shame of the Cities.* New York: McClure, Phillips & Co., 1904.

———. *Lincoln Steffens Speaking.* New York: Harcourt, Brace & Co., 1936.

———. *The Struggle for Self-Government. Being an Attempt to Trace American Political Corruption to Its Sources in Six States of the United States.* New York: McClure, Phillips & Co., 1906.

———. *Upbuilders.* New York: Doubleday, Page & Co., 1909.

Sullivan, Mark. *The Education of an American.* New York: Doubleday, Doran & Co., 1938.

Tarbell, Ida M. *All in the Day's Work. An Autobiography.* New York: Macmillan Co., 1939.

Weinberg, Arthur and Lila (eds.). *The Muckrakers.* New York: Simon & Schuster, 1961.

EUGENE VICTOR DEBS

"Application for Pardon of Eugene V. Debs. Letter from the Attorney General (H. M. Daugherty) to the President in the Matter of the Application for Pardon in Behalf of Eugene V. Debs." Washington: Government Printing Office, 1922.

Coleman, McAlister. *Eugene V. Debs: A Man Unafraid.* New York: Greenberg, 1930.

Debs, Eugene Victor. *Walls and Bars.* Chicago: Socialist Party, 1927.

———. *Writings and Speeches of . . .* Introduction by Arthur M. Schlesinger, Jr. New York: Hermitage Press, Inc., 1948.

Ginger, Ray. *The Bending Cross. A Biography of Eugene Victor Debs.* New Brunswick, N.J.: Rutgers University Press, 1949.

Karsner, David. *Debs. His Authorized Life and Letters from Woodstock Prison to Atlanta.* New York: Boni & Liveright, 1919.

Lapworth, Charles. "The Tour of the Red Special." *International Socialist Review* 9, no. 6 (December 1908) :401–15.

"Eugene V. Debs, the 'Gentle Hoosier Socialist.' " *Literary Digest* 91, no. 7 (November 13, 1926): 40–46.

Morgan, H. Wayne. *Eugene V. Debs. Socialist for President.* Syracuse, N.Y.: Syracuse University Press, 1962.

Sinclair, Upton. *Debs and the Poets.* Pasadena, Calif.: author, 1920.

Thomas, Norman. "Eugene Victor Debs." *New York Times Current History* 25 (December 1926): 373–76.

CLARENCE SEWARD DARROW

Darrow, Clarence. *An Eye for an Eye.* Girard, Kan.: Haldeman–Julius Co., ca. 1905.

———. *Farmington.* Chicago: A. C. McClurg & Co., 1904.

———. *A Persian Pearl and Other Essays.* Chicago: C. L. Ricketts, 1902.

———. *Resist Not Evil.* Chicago: C. H. Kerr & Co., 1903.

———. *The Story of My Life.* New York: Charles Scribner's Sons, 1932.

——— and Wallace Rice. *Infidels and Heretics: An Agnostic's Anthology.*

Harrison, Charles Yale. *Clarence Darrow.* New York: Jonathan Cape & Harrison Smith, 1931.

Ravitz, Abe C. *Clarence Darrow and the American Literary Tradition.* Cleveland: Press of Western Reserve University, 1962.

Stone, Irving. *Clarence Darrow for the Defense.* Garden City, N.Y.: Doubleday, Doran & Co., 1941.

Weinberg, Arthur (ed.). *Attorney for the Damned. Clarence Darrow in His Own Words.* New York: Simon & Schuster, 1957.

Weinberg, Arthur and Lila (eds.). *Verdicts Out of Court.* Chicago: Quadrangle Books, 1963.

JOHN PETER ALTGELD

Altgeld, John P. *The Cost of Something for Nothing.* Chicago: Hammersmark Publishing Co., 1904.

———. *Live Questions, Comprising His Papers, Speeches and Interviews; Also His Messages to the Legislature of Illinois, and a Statement of the Facts Which Influenced His Course As Governor on Several Famous Occasions.* Chicago: George B. Brown & Son, 1899.

———. *Oratory, Its Requirements and Its Rewards.* Chicago: Charles H. Kerr & Co., 1901.

"John Peter Altgeld." *The Public* 4, no. 207 (March 22, 1902): 786–91.

Barnard, Harry. *Eagle Forgotten. The Life of John*

Peter Altgeld. New York and Indianapolis: Bobbs–Merrill Co., 1938.

Brown, Edward Osgood. "Biographical Sketch of Hon. John Peter Altgeld, Twentieth Governor of Illinois." Read before the Chicago Historical Society, December 5, 1905.

Browne, Waldo R. *Altgeld of Illinois. A Record of His Life and Work.* New York: B. W. Huebsch, Inc., 1924.

Chicago Martyrs. *The Famous Speeches of the Eight Anarchists in Judge Gary's Court, October 7, 8, 9, 1886.* San Francisco: Free Society Publishers, 1899.

Christman, Henry M. (ed.). *The Mind and Spirit of John Peter Altgeld.* Urbana: University of Illinois Press, 1960.

Ginger, Ray. *Altgeld's America. The Lincoln Ideal versus Changing Realities.* New York: Funk & Wagnalls Co., 1958.

Holly, William H. "A Forgotten Governor." A paper prepared for and read to the Chicago Literary Club, October 31, 1932. Published by Friends of Governor Altgeld.

Kraus, Adolf. *Reminiscences and Comments.* Chicago: Toby Rubovitz, Inc., 1925.

Masters, Edgar Lee. "John Peter Altgeld." *American Mercury* 4, no. 14 (February 1929): 161–74.

JANE ADDAMS

Addams, Jane. *Democracy and Social Ethics.* New York: Macmillan Co., 1902.

———. *The Excellent Becomes the Permanent.* New York: Macmillan Co., 1932.

———. *The Long Road of Woman's Memory.* New York: Macmillan Co., 1916.

———. *New Conscience and an Ancient Evil.* New York: Macmillan Co., 1912.

———. *Newer Ideals of Peace.* New York: Macmillan Co., 1907.

———. *Peace and Bread.* New York: Macmillan Co., 1922.

———. *The Second Twenty Years at Hull-House, September 1909 to September 1929.* New York: Macmillan Co., 1930.

———. *The Spirit of Youth and the City Streets.* New York: Macmillan Co., 1909.

———. *Twenty Years at Hull-House, With Autobiographical Notes.* New York: Macmillan Co., 1910.

———. *Women at The Hague. The International Congress of Women and Its Results.* New York: Macmillan Co., 1915.

——— and Ellen G. Starr. *Hull-House: A Social Settlement. An Outline Sketch.* February 1, 1894 (no publisher given).

Conway, Jill. "Jane Addams: An American Heroine." *Daedalus* 93, no. 2 (Spring 1964) :761–80.

Farrell, John C. *Beloved Lady. A History of Jane Addams' Ideas on Reform and Peace.* Baltimore: The Johns Hopkins Press, 1967.

Linn, James Weber. *Jane Addams. A Biography.* New York: D. Appleton–Century Co., 1935.

Taylor, Graham. "Jane Addams: The Great Neighbor." *Survey Graphic* 24, no. 7, (July 1935) :338–41, 68.

Wise, Winifred E. *Jane Addams of Hull-House. A Biography.* New York: Harcourt, Brace & Co., 1935.

ROBERT GREEN INGERSOLL

Braden, Clark. *Ingersoll Unmasked. A Scathing and Fearless Exposé of His Real Life.* Lexington, Ky.: Blue Grass Printing Co., 1900.

Cramer, Clarence H. *Royal Bob. The Life of Robert G. Ingersoll.* New York and Indianapolis: Bobbs–Merrill Co., 1952.

Debs, Eugene Victor. *Pastels of Men.* New York: Pearson's Library, 1919.

Dement, R. S. *Ingersoll, Beecher, and Dogma.* Chicago: S. C. Griggs & Co., 1878.

Field, Henry. "An Open Letter to Robert G. Ingersoll." *North American Review* 145 (August 1887): 128–45.

Field, Henry. "A Last Word to Robert G. Ingersoll." *North American Review* 145 (December 1887): 616–28.

Ingersoll, Robert G. *The Letters of . . .* Edited and with a Biographical Introduction by Eva Ingersoll Wakefield. New York: Philosophical Library, 1951.

———. "Letter to Dr. Field." *North American Review* 146 (January 1888) :31–46.

———. "A Reply to the Rev. Henry M. Field." *North*

American Review 145 (November 1887):473–505.

———. *The Writings of . . .* (12 vols.) New York: Dresden Publishing Co., 1900.

Kittredge, Herman E. *Ingersoll. A Biographical Appreciation.* New York: Dresden Publishing Co., 1911.

Lambert, L. A., Rev. *Notes on Ingersoll.* Buffalo, N.Y.: Buffalo Catholic Publication Co., 1886.

Larson, Orvin. *American Infidel: Robert G. Ingersoll.* New York: Citadel Press, 1962.

Roberts, Cameron. *Colonel Bob Ingersoll. A Biographical Narrative of the Great American Orator and Agnostic.* Garden City, N.Y.: Doubleday, Page & Co., 1927.

Smith, Edward Garstin. *The Life and Reminiscences of Robert G. Ingersoll.* New York: National Weekly Publishing Co., 1904.

Stevenson, Adlai E. *Something of Men I Have Known, With Some Papers of a General Nature, Political, Historic, and Retrospective.* Chicago: A. C. McClurg & Co., 1909.

GENERAL

Aaron, Daniel. *Men of Good Hope. A Story of American Progressives.* New York: Oxford University Press, 1951.

Adamic, Louis. *Dynamite: The Story of Class Violence in America.* New York: Viking Press, 1931, 1934.

Beard, Charles A. and Mary R. *The Rise of American Civilization.* New York: Macmillan Co., 1935.

Suggested Readings

Filler, Louis. *Crusaders for American Liberalism.* New York: Harcourt, Brace & Co., 1939.

Goldberg, Harvey (ed.). *American Radicals. Some Problems and Personalities.* New York: Monthly Review Press, 1957.

Goldman, Eric F. *Rendezvous with Destiny.* New York: Alfred A. Knopf, 1953.

Lasch, Christopher. *The New Radicalism in America, 1889–1963. The Intellectual As a Social Type.* New York: Alfred A. Knopf, 1965.

Lerner, Max. *America as a Civilization. Life and Thought in the United States Today.* New York: Simon & Schuster, 1957.

Link, Arthur S. *American Epoch. A History of the United States Since the 1890's.* New York: Alfred A. Knopf, 1955.

Madison, Charles A. *Critics and Crusaders. A Century of American Protest.* New York: Henry Holt & Co., 1947.

INDEX

Addams, Anna Haldeman, 151, 153
Addams Center, 174
Addams Guard, 150-51
Addams, Jane, 14, 127, 133, 144, 149-74, 207; background, 150 ff.; in Europe, 152 ff.; founds Hull-House, 154 ff.; and sanitation, 157 ff.; and labor unions, 159; in 1905 teamster strike, 160; campaigns for T. Roosevelt in 1912, 164; at International Congress of Women, 165; proposes continuous mediation, 165-66; reports on Peace Delegation, 166 ff.; a founder of ACLU, 168; defends conscientious objectors, 168; "Pacifism and Patriotism," 168; awarded Nobel Peace prize, 170; honored by Women's International League, 171; supports Herbert Hoover in 1932, 171; on internationalism, 172; dies, 173
Addams, John, 150-51
Addams, Sarah, 151
Age of Reason, The, 179, 185
Agnosticism, 99, 193, 205
Altgeld, Emma Ford, 132, 144
Altgeld, John, 128
Altgeld, John P. (Gov.), 14, 15, 36, 68, 72, 94, 121-45, 159, 207; and Pres. Cleveland, 69, 136 ff.; Haymarket pardon, 124 ff.; background, 127 ff.; *Oratory*, 132; Unity Building, 132-33; elected judge, 133-34; *Our Penal Machinery*, 134-35; elected governor, 136; government by injunction, 138-39; University of Illinois, 139-40; defeated for second term, 140; runs for Chicago mayor, defeated, 142-43; at 1900 Democratic convention, 142; joins Darrow law firm, 143; defends Boers, 143-44; dies, 144
Amalgamated Clothing Workers of America, 171
Amalgamated Woodworkers' International Union, 98
American Appeal, 82
American Civil Liberties Union, 168
American Fed. of Labor, 40, 75
American Magazine, 32, 37
American Mercury, 115
American Railway Union, 68, 72, 96, 136, 159
American Revolution, 185
American Union Against Militarism, 168
Anarchism, 13, 19, 44, 90, 122, 123
Anthony, Susan B., 63
Anti-evolution law, 107 ff.
Appeal to Reason, 40
Arbeiter Zeitung, 122
Arlington National Cemetery, 204
Autobiography of Lincoln Steffens, The, 47-48

Baker, Newton D., 170
Baker, Ray Stannard, 30, 35, 37
Bakunin, Michael, 13
Barrymore, Maurice, 202
Berger, Victor L., 70-71
Black man, 15, 73-74, 111 ff., 189
Black, William P., 195
Blaine, James G., 188, 189
Boers case, 143-44
Bolshevik, 46, 50, 83
Bonfield, John, 122
Bontecou, Josephine, 23, 50
Brotherhood of Locomotive Firemen, 63, 64, 65
Brown, Edward Osgood, 131
Bryan, William Jennings, 55, 57, 107, 108, 140, 142, 145

Index

Bull Moose party, 59
Bullitt, William C., 45
Bunyan, John, 36
Burns, Robert, 100, 178, 182
Butler, Nicholas Murray, 170
Byron, 182

Cannon, Joseph G., 33
Carnegie, Andrew, 202
Carranza, Venustiano, 44
Carter, Orrin (Justice), 107, 168
Caverly, John R. (Judge), 89, 92
Chicago & Northwestern Ry., 69, 96
Chicago *Evening American*, 100
Chicago *Evening Post*, 101
Chicago, Milwaukee & St. Paul Ry., 96
Chicago *Tribune*, 145, 203
Christianity, 19, 38, 198
Civil War, 11, 128, 150, 186-87
Cleveland, Grover (Pres.), 68, 136 ff., 139
Colby, Everett, 34
Cole, Fay-Cooper, 109
Collective bargaining, 12
Collier's, 32, 115
Commercial Advertiser, 27-28
Communist party, 46, 50, 83
Comte, 182
Cook County Juvenile Court, 157
Corruption, 19, 26, 30, 32
Cosmopolitan, 32, 35, 36
Cowper, 182
"Creed of Science," 204
Cregier, DeWitt C., 95
Crocker, Richard, 141
"Cross of Gold," 57
Culver, Helen, 154, 155
Curie, Marie, 111
Curtis, Winterton C., 109

Darrow, Amirus, 92
Darrow Center, 174
Darrow, Clarence S., 14, 15, 19, 40, 41-43, 72, 78, 87-117, 123, 127, 134, 143, 144, 149, 159, 162, 192, 204, 207; Debs case, 69, 96; Leopold and Loeb, 87 ff.; background, 92 ff.; at Free Trade convention, 95; on conspiracy law, 97; Kidd, 98-99; *Resist Not Evil*, 100; *Farmington*, 100; *An Eye for an Eye*, 100; *A Persian Pearl*, 100; United Mine Workers, 101; Haywood, Moyer, Pettibone, 103; McNamara, 103 ff.; charged with bribery, 104; Communists, 106-7; *Crime: Its Causes and Treatment*, 107; Scopes, 107 ff.; examines Bryan, 109 ff.; Sweet, 111 ff.; defends black man, 111; *Story of My Life*, 115; articles, 115; heads NRA Review Board, 115-16; dies, 117
Darrow, Emily, 92
Darrow, Paul, 101
Darwin, Charles, 12, 107, 193
Das Kapital, 70
Dayton case, 12, 107 ff.
Death of Socrates, 182
Debs, Eugene Victor, 14, 15, 39, 45, 55-84, 96-97, 136, 159, 207; background, 59 ff.; Socialist party presidential candidate (1900), 72-73; (1908), 55-58; (1920), 59, 80-81; on Ingersoll, 62; Brotherhood of Locomotive Firemen, 64, 66; American Railway Union, 67; tried for criminal conspiracy, 69-70; convicted for violating injunction, 70; becomes a Socialist, 71; defends Pullman strike, 71-72; campaigns for Bryan (1896), 72; on the Negro, 73-74; "Negro and His Nemesis," 74; helps found IWW, 75; opposes World War I, 76; convicted of violating Espionage Act, 78-82; dies, 83
Debs, Jean Daniel, 59-60
Debs, Kate Metzel, 66, 71, 82
Debs, Marguerite Bettrich, 59, 60-61
Debs, Theodore, 64, 71, 82
"Declaration of the Free," 204
Democratic party, 59, 76, 142, 143
Department of Justice (U.S.), 78
Depew, Chauncey, 36, 37, 202
"Does Man Have Free Will?", 115
"Does Man Live Again?", 115
Dorsey brothers, 194
Douglas, Stephen, 185
Douglass, Frederick, 189-90
Dunne, Finley Peter, 37

"Eagle Forgotten, An," 145
Eliot, George, 156
Emancipation Proclamation, 187
Emerson, Ralph Waldo, 13
Engel, George, 123, 124
Epicurus, 182
Espionage Act, 78
Establishment, 13, 15, 48

Index

Everybody's Magazine, 32, 37
Evolution, 12, 107, 193
Eye for an Eye, An, 100

Farmington, 100
Fascism, 49
Federal troops, to Chicago, 68
Field, Eugene, and Debs, 69
Field, Henry M., and Ingersoll, 199 ff.
Fielden, Samuel, 123, 124, 126
Fifer, Joseph W. (Gov.), 124
Fischer, Adolph, 123, 124
Fischer, Kuno, 22
Folk, Joseph W., 23-30
Food Administration, 169
Ford, Emma, 132
Ford, Henry, "peace ship," 167
Franks, Robert, 88 ff.
"Free-thought," 196
Free Trade convention, 95
Frenzied Finance, 32
Fundamentalist, 12, 108

Gage, Lyman J., 123
"Gateway, The," 49, 51
Geisler, Jerry, 104
General Assembly of Indiana, 84
General Managers Assn., 97
George, Henry, 38, 94
Gladstone, William E., 200
Godwin, 138
Goethe, 60
"Golden Rule," 41, 43
Gompers, Samuel, 40
Great American Fraud, The, 32
Great Northern Ry., 67, 68
Greeley, Horace, 61
Gridiron Club, 36

Haldeman, Anna, 151, 153
Haldeman, George, 151, 153
Hamerstrom, Ruby, 101
Hampton's, 32
Harding, Warren G. (Pres.), 81
Harper's Weekly, 24
Harrison, Carter H., Jr. (Mayor), 141, 142
Harrison, Carter H., Sr. (Mayor), 122
Haymarket affair, 14, 15, 121 ff., 124, 127, 129, 136, 139, 162, 195
Haywood, William D., 75, 102
Hearst, William Randolph, 100
Hegel, 22
Hillman, Sidney, 171
"History of Standard Oil," 31
Holly, William (Judge), 117
Holy Roller meeting, 111
Hoover, Herbert (Pres.), 169, 170
Hopkins, Samuel Adams, 32
House of Representatives (U.S.), 36
Howells, William Dean, 123
Hubbard, Elbert, 202
Hughes, Charles Evans, 167
Hugo, Victor, 60
Hull, Charles J., 154
Hull-House, 139, 149, 155-63, 165, 169, 173, 174
Huxley, Thomas, 193, 201

Ickes, Harold, 171
Illinois Supreme Court, 107
Illinois Senate, 173
Imperialism, 142
Independent, 32
Industrial Workers of the World (IWW), 75
Ingersoll, Ebon Clark, 179, 183, 185, 192
Ingersoll, John, 178, 179-80
Ingersoll, John, Jr., 179
Ingersoll, "Priest," 178, 179-80
Ingersoll, Robert G., 14, 15, 61, 62, 65, 95, 123, 177-205, 207; "Liberty of Man, Woman, and Child," 62, 180; background, 178 ff.; on traditional religion, 181-82; on his father, 182; opens law office, 183; on baptism, 183; on Thomas Paine, 184-85; denies inspiration of Scriptures, 185; candidate for U.S. Congress, defeated, 185, 186; "Fugitive Slave Law," 186; Colonel, 187; on Lincoln, 187; becomes active Republican, 187 ff.; loses in race for governor, 188; nominates Blaine, 188-89; on the Negro, 189; "Vision of War," 190; "Soliloquy at the Tomb of Napoleon," 191; "The Gods," 192; "Mistakes of Moses," 193; "Orthodoxy," 193; and Darwin, 193; attacks literal interpretation of Bible, 194; Star Routes case, 194 ff.; invited to join Haymarket defense, 195; defines blasphemy, 197-98; on Christianity, 199-201; on Walt Whitman, 201-2; "What Is Religion?", 202-3; on death, 203; dies, 203
International Assn. of Bridge and Structural Workers (AFL), 40

Index

International Congress of Women, 165
International Socialist Review, 73
Isaak, Abraham, 162-63
"Is Civilization a Failure?", 115
"Is Life Worth Living?", 115
Isolationism, 11

Jackson, Andrew (Pres.), 11
Jackson Park, Chicago, 87, 116
Jacobs, Aletta, 165-66
Jefferson, Thomas (Pres.), 13, 93
Jewish Lower East Side, 25
Johns Hopkins University, 153
Jungle, The, 32

Kellogg, William B., 185, 186
Kelly, Florence, 139
Keyser, Mary, 155
Khayyam, Omar, 99, 100, 101
Kidd, Thomas I., 98, 99
Koht, Halvan, 170
Kropotkin, Peter, 13, 90, 162
Krudewolf, Johann Friedrich, 27

Labor unions, in Hull-House, 159
Lackawanna Railroad, 28
LaFollette, Robert M., 33
Laissez faire, 12
Lanehart, Mary, 128
Lathrop, Julia, 157, 173
League of Nations, 169, 172
Leaves of Grass, 201
Lenin, N., 45, 46
Leopold, Nathan, Jr., 87 ff., 107
Lexow committee, 26
"Liberty of Man, Woman, and Child," 180
Lincoln, Abraham (Pres.), 74, 151, 187
Lindsay, Vachel, 145
Lindsey, Benjamin B. (Judge), 34
Lingg, Louis, 123, 124
Lippmann, Walter, 37
Livingston, Mary, 179
Livingston, Robert R., 179
Loeb, Richard, 87 ff., 107
London School of Economics, 46
Los Angeles *Times*, 38, 39, 40, 103

McClure's Magazine, 28 ff., 37
McClure, S. S., 28, 30, 31-32
McKinley, William (Pres.), 162
McNamara case, 38-43, 103 ff.
Madison Square Presbyterian Church, 25
Magazine, The, 63, 64
Manning, Henry E. (Cardinal), 200
Marlowe, Julia, 202
Marx, Karl, 13, 70, 71
Mather, Kirtley F., 109
Metcalf, Maynard, 109
Metzel, Katherine, 65
Mexican revolution, 44, 45
Mezuzah, 25
Molière, 60
Moses in Red, 47
Most, John, 13
Moyer, Charles H., 102
Muckrakers, 12, 32, 35, 36, 48
Mussolini, 46, 47-48

Nation, 138
National Assn. for the Advancement of Colored People, 113
National Fed. of Settlements, 169
National Recovery Admin., 115-16
Nazism, 49
Neebe, Oscar, 123, 126
Negrò (*see* Black man)
"Negro and His Nemesis," 74
New Testament, 38
New York Evangelist, 199
New York *Evening Post*, 24 ff.
New York police, 25
New York *Sun*, 126-27
New York Times, 81, 100
New York *Tribune*, 61
New York *World*, 127
Nihilist, 15
Nobel Peace prize, 170
Norris-LaGuardia Act, 139
North American Review, 199

Occidental Literary Club, 61-63
Oglesby, Richard (Gov.), 124, 188
Ohio National Guard, 128
Ohio Socialist convention, 77
Ohl, Jessie, 93
Old Testament, 26
"Open Letter to Robert G. Ingersoll," 199
Orchard, Harry, 102
Oskar II, "peace ship," 167
Our Penal Machinery and Its Victims, 134 ff.
Otis, Harrison Gray, 39

Paine, George, 99
Paine Lumber Co., 98, 99
Paine, Thomas, 61, 93, 111, 178, 179, 182, 184

Index

Palmer, A. Mitchell, 170
Palmer, John M., 188
Panic of 1893, 27, 67
Parker, Benjamin Weld, 186
Parker, Eva, 186
Parkhurst, Charles (Rev.), 25
Parsons, Albert R., 123, 124
"Peace ship," 167
Pershing, John J. (Gen.), 170
Persian Pearl and Others Essays, 100
Petrarch, 182
Pettibone, George, 102
Phillips, David Graham, 35-36
Phillips, Wendell, 63
Philosophical Dictionary, 61
Pilgrim's Progress, 36
Plato's *Death of Socrates*, 182
Populism, 12
Populist party, 73
Presidential elections: (1876), 188-89; (1892), 36; (1896), 140; (1900), 59; (1904), 59; (1908), 59; (1912), 59; (1916), 76, 167; (1920), 59, 80-81
Progress and Poverty, 94
Progressive party, 59, 164
Progressivism, 12
Prohibition, 12
Pujo Committee (Senate), 32
Pullman, George, 67, 97, 159
Pullman Palace Car Co., 17, 67-68, 96, 137, 159
Pure Food and Drug Act, 32

Racine, 60
"Red raids," 169
Red Special, 55-57, 58
Reform, Age of, 12
Republican party, 164, 188, 189, 194
Resist Not Evil, 100
Reynolds, Charles B., 195 ff.
"Right to Work," 30
Riley, James Whitcomb, 63
Rogers, Earl, 104
Romola, 156
Roosevelt, Eleanor, 171
Roosevelt, Franklin D. (Pres.), 11, 12, 116, 171
Roosevelt, Theodore (Pres.), 26-27, 35-37, 57, 59, 101, 164, 184
Russia, 44, 45, 46, 48, 83

Schmittberger, Max, 26
Schwab, Michael, 123, 124, 126
Scopes, John T., 12, 107 ff.
Securities Act of 1933, 32
Seidl, Anton, 202
Shakespeare, 178, 182
"Shame of Minneapolis," 30
Shame of the Cities, The, 33
Shelley, 182
Sherman Anti-Trust Act, 69
Sigma Delta Chi, 51
Sinclair, Upton, 32
Single Tax, 38
Single Tax Club, 94
Sissman, Peter, 106
Smith College, 152
Social Democratic party, 72
Socialism, 13, 38, 74
Socialist party, 72, 74, 80, 83; presidential campaign (1900), (1904), (1912), 59; (1908), 55 ff.; (1920), 59, 80-81
Socrates, 182
Sorbonne, 23
Soviet Union, 44, 45, 46, 48, 83
Spanish-American War, 11, 142
Spanish Civil War, 49
Spencer, Herbert, 193
Spies, August, 122, 123, 124
Spreckels, Rudolph, 34
Stanton, Elizabeth Cody, 202
Starr, Ellen Gates, 152, 153 ff.
Steffens, Joseph, 20
Steffens, Lincoln, 14, 15, 19-51, 55, 116-17, 207; on anarchism, 19; on life, 20; on privileges, 20, 30; on corruption, 20, 50; background, 21 ff.; as reporter, 24 ff.; "almost a Jew," 25-26; *Commercial Advertiser*, 27-28; *McClure's Magazine*, 28 ff., 37; on bribery, 30, 43; "Tweed Days in St. Louis," 30, 35; "The Shame of Minneapolis," 30; on LaFollette's Wisconsin, 33; "The Shame of the Cities," 33; *Struggle for Self-Government*, 34; *Upbuilders*, 34; *American Magazine*, 37; *Everybody's Magazine*, 37; on Christianity, 38, 40-41; as Darrow witness, 41-43; on social crime, 42-43; on free speech, 44; Mexican revolution, 44; on Russia, 45-46; *Moses in Red*, 47; *Autobiography*, 47-48; on universities, 49; on Spain, 49; "The Gateway," 49, 51; *Steffens Speaking*, 50; dies, 50
Stockyards, Chicago, 32
Struggle for Self-Government, The, 34

Stürgkh, prime minister of Austria, 166
Sue, Eugène, 60
Sullivan, Mark, 32, 35
Sumner, William Graham, 193
Superstition, 15
Sweat shops, 160
Sweet case, 111 ff.
Symes, Elizabeth Louisa, 21

Taft, William Howard (Pres.), 55, 57, 164
Tammany Hall, 25, 31, 141
Tarbell, Ida, 31, 35, 37
Tennessee Supreme Court, 110
Thomas, Norman, 84
Thoreau, Henry David, 13
Tolstoy, Leo, 99
Torah, 26
"Treason of the Senate," 35
Twain, Mark, 204
"Tweed Days in St. Louis," 30, 35

United Mine Workers, 101
United States Supreme Court, 80, 124
Unity Building, 132-33
University of Chicago, 87, 117
University of Illinois, 139-40; Circle Campus, 174
University of Michigan, 87
University of Wisconsin, 158
Upbuilders, 34
U'Ren, W. S., 34

Vanity Fair, 115
Veteran Soldiers of the Rebellion, 190
Voltaire, 60, 93, 111, 178, 182

Waldheim Cemetery, 195
Wall Street, 24-25, 27
Warren, Josiah, 13
Washington, George (Pres.), 179
Water Works Improvement Assn., 112
Western Fed. of Miners, 75, 102
Wetmore, Claude H., 29-30
Weyerhauser, 29
White House, 35, 36-37, 177
White, William Allen, 37
Whitlock, Brand, 55
Whitman, Walt, 100, 201
Wilson, Woodrow (Pres.), 59, 76, 81, 164, 167
Winter, Ella, 50
Women's International League for Peace and Freedom, 169, 171
Women's Medical College, 152
Women's Peace party, 165
Women's suffrage, 12
World Court, 172
World War I, 11, 44, 76-77, 81, 106, 169
World War II, 11, 49
Wundt, Wilhelm, 23

Yerkes, Charles T., 133

ABOUT THE AUTHORS

Arthur Weinberg created the bestseller *Attorney for the Damned.* He and his wife Lila have collaborated on a number of books: *The Muckrakers, Verdicts Out of Court, Instead of Violence,* and *Passport to Utopia.* They have also written articles for *Saturday Review, Ebony,* the *Chicago Tribune, Chicago Daily News,* and *Chicago Sun Times.*

Lila Weinberg is currently a manuscript editor at the University of Chicago Press, while Arthur Weinberg is a staff writer for Fairchild Publications. The Weinbergs live in Chicago's Hyde Park with their three teenage daughters.